CRUSHMORE

CRUSHMORE

ESSAYS ON LOVE, LOSS, AND COMING-OF-AGE

PENN BADGLEY, SOPHIE ANSARI, AND NAVA KAVELIN

G
GALLERY BOOKS
NEW YORK   AMSTERDAM/ANTWERP   LONDON
TORONTO   SYDNEY/MELBOURNE   NEW DELHI

G

Gallery Books
An Imprint of Simon & Schuster, LLC
1230 Avenue of the Americas
New York, NY 10020

For more than 100 years, Simon & Schuster has championed authors and the stories they create. By respecting the copyright of an author's intellectual property, you enable Simon & Schuster and the author to continue publishing exceptional books for years to come. We thank you for supporting the author's copyright by purchasing an authorized edition of this book.

No amount of this book may be reproduced or stored in any format, nor may it be uploaded to any website, database, language-learning model, or other repository, retrieval, or artificial intelligence system without express permission. All rights reserved. Inquiries may be directed to Simon & Schuster, 1230 Avenue of the Americas, New York, NY 10020 or permissions@simonandschuster.com.

Copyright © 2025 by Podcrushed, LLC

All rights reserved, including the right to reproduce this book or portions thereof in any form whatsoever. For information, address Gallery Books Subsidiary Rights Department, 1230 Avenue of the Americas, New York, NY 10020.

First Gallery Books hardcover edition October 2025

GALLERY BOOKS and colophon are registered trademarks of Simon & Schuster, LLC

Simon & Schuster strongly believes in freedom of expression and stands against censorship in all its forms. For more information, visit BooksBelong.com.

For information about special discounts for bulk purchases, please contact Simon & Schuster Special Sales at 1-866-506-1949 or business@simonandschuster.com.

The Simon & Schuster Speakers Bureau can bring authors to your live event. For more information or to book an event, contact the Simon & Schuster Speakers Bureau at 1-866-248-3049 or visit our website at www.simonspeakers.com.

The names of some people and places described in the book have been changed.

Interior design by Hope Herr-Cardillo

Manufactured in the United States of America

10 9 8 7 6 5 4 3 2 1

Library of Congress Control Number: 2025940546

ISBN 978-1-6680-7799-3
ISBN 978-1-6680-7801-3 (ebook)

CONTENTS

Introduction ix
Dancing with Myself 1
Hair 23
I Wasn't Meant for the NFL 33
Max Becker: Certified Hottie 43
On a Wednesday 53
In Camera 65
A Family Recipe 89
Cool Girl 97
Forty Days and Forty Nights 109
Devil Worshipper 123
In Her Orbit 129
The Middle 137
Love from Brooklyn 145
los(s) 159
Grief 163
I Love Love 183
The Imaginationship 197
Where Did My Family Go? 211

Lineage 227
After the World Stopped Spinning 237
Decision Day 251
This Is Where We Say Goodbye 259
Acknowledgments 263

To our twelve-year-old selves:
you did the best you could.

INTRODUCTION

Welcome to your orientation.

My name is Penn, and of the three narrative voices shouting into the void for the length of this essay compilation, mine has been chosen for its celebrity and other superior attributes to introduce our readers to *Crushmore* (an opaque and otherwise questionable title).

Let's start at the beginning, like any good genesis story does. I am as famous as I am uneducated. I have spent my adult life starring as the titular character in two large and successful television franchises (*Gossip Girl* and *You*), and yet I didn't finish middle school. My coauthors, on the other hand, are both former middle school teachers who have lived lives of an obscurity so tragic, so unknown, that their written expression here may well read like the entries of a diary from ancient Mesopotamia, only pithier. This is also why I chose them to cohost my podcast in 2022. Together, we launched *Podcrushed* to explore adolescence with celebrity guests—because the world needs now more than ever to hear from celebrities about their experiences and opinions, and because horror stories from adolescence can cure cancer and unite us all.

I am sincere on half of that last point. During adolescence, your sense of identity is transforming like no other period in life. Exiting childhood, a terribly long way from adulthood (not a girl, not yet a woman), you're there for what may as well be the rest of time. For the young person living through it, the only evidence it'll ever end is the world of puttering adults surrounding you who are just so *stupid*. It's hard to be young, and Jane Fonda agrees.

I know this because she told Julia Louis-Dreyfus the exact same thing, who then told me IRL while we interviewed her about her own adolescence on *Podcrushed*. Not thirty minutes later—this is true—I was doing the Elaine dance in front of Julia, who remained civil and kind through the entire fifteen seconds (which are now immortalized on TikTok). I believe she tolerated it mostly because she was on a press cycle, but partly because she really enjoyed our conversation reflecting on her youth. Otherwise, those fifteen seconds could have been fantastically uncomfortable for me, alone with Julia in the New York studios while Sophie and Nava recorded remotely (safely) from Los Angeles. For the first season of *Podcrushed*, every time I had to ask our guests to film a TikTok, I had a deep-seated (or is it deep-seeded?) fear that it would be poorly received, that our guest would become irked or offended, and that I would humiliate myself. Every time, I felt like I was in the fifth grade again, asking Kayla Petersen to the movies over spring break—which I did—and that she would reject me—which she did. Season 1 *Podcrushed* TikToks felt like the first time, every time.

Peak middle-school vibes.

INTRODUCTION

So, by now we've established that my show—sorry, *our* show—focuses on adolescence. We'll get to the why in a little bit. But let's spend a little more time on the what by evoking the WHO.

The World Health Organization identifies adolescence as the period of ten to nineteen years old, while the *Oxford* definition offers a concise one-liner that we at *Podcrushed* find emotionally violent: "The period following the onset of puberty during which a young person develops from a child into an adult."

Shaking my head at *Oxford*. Shaking my damn head.

Think of what's happening! The vast expanses of the intelligent mind and perception that will develop; the emotions (the feels) that will deepen, vivify, and then guide behavior; the procreative and sexual powers of the body that simply do not exist until, suddenly, they do. When we recall this period of life after having traversed it, we may appreciate that it is a time of first after first after first.

First crush. First heartbreak. First period.

First dance. First love.* First fight.

First loss. First cigarette. First dead body.

Sorry, those last two are grafted from *Stand by Me*, the Rob Reiner–directed American adolescent classic, which many people remember nostalgically as a perfect film. The seductive archetypes of youth! Charming boys who curse and say things about girls they've heard grown men say! They smoke, dodge trains,

---

* It bears mentioning that as authors we experienced some of these firsts as adults. A few of the essays are written from a (mostly) adult perspective, one which appreciates how the formative experiences of puberty could be poking their grubby little fingers into our adult lives and shaping things for us in ways we might not have appreciated until we wrote these essays.

solve murders, and get leeches on their scrotums! Typical for any thirteen-year-old.

In the Wikipedia entry for the film, you'll find an interesting hyperlink: *coming-of-age stories*. There, *Stand by Me* stands alongside a lengthy list of timeless and gargantuan titles of literature, many of which are still bangers but not necessarily obvious choices for coming-of-age tales:

- *The Telemachy* in Homer's *Odyssey* from the eighth century BC (love it want it need it)
- *Candide* by Voltaire from 1759 which, candide-ly, flopped and pissed people off
- *Little Women* ever heard of *Little Men*? Exactly
- *The Virgin Suicides*, which should not sound so sexy but
- *Oliver Twist* meh but technically full of child prostitutes and criminals
- *The Adventures of Tom Sawyer* and *Adventures of Huckleberry Finn* not aging well, sorry, Mark
- *The Catcher in the Rye* featuring the OG Dan Humphrey (IYKYK)
- *The Jungle Book* is a coming-of-age story idk
- *Harry Potter*
- *The Sisterhood of the Traveling Pants*
- *Winter's Bone* joke redacted bc I'm not still twelve
- *Life of Pi* (*Jungle Book* on a boat)
- *Call Me by Your Name* starring Timmy Chalamet (love)
- *East of Eden* starring James Dean (the Timmy Chalamet of 1955)
- *To Kill a Mockingbird* no joke

INTRODUCTION

- *The Graduate*
- *It*
- *A Clockwork Orange*

You can see that the list ranges from archaic to postmodern, from wholesome antics to rape and murder, and in one case, a prepubescent orgy (we didn't write it!). The spectrum is a wide one, and although we draw the line way before you get to prepubescent orgy, we otherwise revel in a true diversity of perspectives and experience. After nearly hundreds of hours of interviews, we are still excited to explore what it means to "come of age." Where, how, and when does it begin? Does it ever end? *Are you okay?*

On *Podcrushed*, we explore all of this with celebrities, experts, and even with our listeners, who number in the many millions (trust us). People like Conan O'Brien, Ariana Grande, Ayo Edebiri, Matthew McConaughey, Jenna Ortega, Kevin Bacon, Eddie Redmayne, Taylor Swift, and former President Barack Obama all have coming-of-age stories to—

Sorry, those last two are grafted from Nava's and Sophie's wish lists. Let them dream.

Not long ago, Nava was a teacher and lectured briefly at Tsinghua University in Beijing. Her stay overlapped with Sophie's, who lived there when she was a senior in high school. Although Nava was never Sophie's teacher (she still refuses), she was witness to Sophie's adolescent mishaps and shenanigans. Nava could roast her mercilessly, but she chooses not to because Sophie could just as easily roast Nava for her *adult* mishaps and shenanigans. Nava is someone for whom middle school's uniquely awkward stage has had no end. She has a Homeric scroll of truly hilarious and painfully embarrassing stories that stretch well into adulthood. As such, Nava and Sophie are bound by a contract of secrecy and mutually assured destruction, which may or may not be written in Mandarin.

While Nava and Sophie were in Beijing, I was nearing the end of my run portraying an iconic high schooler on *Gossip Girl* as a man fully in my midtwenties. It's hard to imagine that, if you are holding this book in your hands, you wouldn't have at least some idea about what—or who—*Gossip Girl* is, but should we try for a synopsis anyhow? Fun! Okay, so assuming I'm not about to have a stroke, it's about a half dozen kids attending an elite private school in the uberwealthy Upper East Side of Manhattan, New York, just before the advent of social media. There is an anonymous blogger who calls herself Gossip Girl and she is the remorseless, secret-stealing, shame-inducing, headline-blasting snitch who broadcasts all the tea about these kids over text for no reason that is ever, ever clear except that she must be very sad and alone. Who is she? Google it.

I met Nava and Sophie in New York City in the years after *Gossip Girl,* while I was growing my hair luxuriously long and playing music like every actor must before they stick to acting. I would, on occasion, consider the broader social implications of a show like the one that had made me famous. Nava was working at the United Nations, and one of her focuses was researching the effects of media on youth. (The data is not terribly encouraging!) Around the same time, I attended a conference whose purpose was, of all things, to engage in serious and hopeful discussions around the unique potential middle schoolers possess to become spearheads of social change in their neighborhoods. (This data is far more encouraging!) It was one of the most inspiring events of my adult life, and Sophie, at a ripe twenty years of age, was a facilitator in one of my breakout groups.

Given our collective context, *Podcrushed* makes sense. But if you had asked me then, "Do you think you'll start a podcast with these two women?" I would have said, "With whom?"

"Sophie Ansari and Nava Kavelin."

"I'm sorry, I'm not taking pictures at this time."

So, here we are. Three best friends about to open the treasure trove of childhood trauma for your enjoyment (maybe) and our growth (hopefully).

Stick around.*

---

* Avid listeners know I hate saying this but have found myself repeating it for something like 97 percent of the introductions to every episode. Why? Because David, our engineer and husband to cohost Sophie, writes the copy for guest intros and evidently thinks we're hosting a Nickelodeon telethon. Love you, David.

DANCING WITH MYSELF

PENN

Los Angeles, 1999.

What I see at twelve years old is the cement arches of LAX's 1960s Space Age Theme Building, and although it's inescapably retro, it's also pretty cool looking. It's nighttime, around nine o'clock, much warmer than any early spring I knew in Washington State. There are palm trees everywhere, swaying slowly and splaying their fronds in a way that is nearly obscene.

LA is exotic; I get it.

In my hands is a silver Sony Discman playing Dru Hill's self-titled debut, which I prefer over their more successful, less self-titled *Enter the Dru*. (Don't be confused; both are bangers.) My headphones are on, and I suppose I'm hearing, subconsciously, my heart's deepest wish in the extreme libidinal desire of Sisqó's tenor—to be known and loved unconditionally, as every human being deserves. This desire transcends sexual communion, maybe even death, but I won't know more about those transcendent dimensions of desire for at least a decade. Right now, this music moves me and if I'm thinking about any sort of death, it is only *la petite mort*. I mean, these palm trees are practically coming on to me.

While Dru Hill are stacking four-part harmonies like bricks and pining after a stone-cold baddie who left Sisqó (the nerve!), I'm standing with my mother waiting for a yellow cab. In my memory, my mother is essentially not there. It's all me. This is integral to the memory. While the normal loneliness or isolation of being an only child had characterized much of my childhood, what I feel at twelve is different. I am now in the world, and in some way, somehow, alone in my journey through it. Maybe I'm suffering the necessary evolution of self-centeredness as my prepubescent consciousness enters the next great chapter of neurological development: I *am* the world (or, if it's only my oyster, then it's finally ready to be shucked). Whatever is causing this new feeling of aloneness, it's proven at least by the fact that before the end of the week I will have seen porn for the first time and had my first kiss during Truth or Dare in a hot tub. Before the end of the summer, I will have gotten drunk and high—separately, each for the first time. One cannot engage thusly while holding one's mother's hand, so to speak. A change is coming.

While I don't know any of that is on the horizon, I can sense I'm at a precipice of some kind. I'm excited and apprehensive, in a new world pulsating with a shadowy thrill. Standing on the curb at Los Angeles International Airport, I'm nearing the end of *Enter the Dru*. This record is such a vibe, and as a chubby kid from the semirural Northwest, when I put headphones on with music like this, I'm gone. I'm in a world of my own imagination and that of my closest confidants and role models, who are pop stars. My pop was R & B, but something about that acronym doesn't capture how huge this music was for me, nor how huge the music was, period. Nineties R & B was titanically popular. It was flashy. It was commercial. It was dancing and singing in the rain with a wet shirt on, calling out for your baby just like the Backstreet Boys and Britney Spears were; it just wasn't so prepubescent in its yearning (though it was equally desperate).

Let's call it what it is: nineties R & B was transparent about how much it wanted to hump, and that's one of only two reasons we don't call it pop music outright. The other is its history as a Black genre, which is legitimate—a book in its own right—but are we really going to call nineties R & B *rhythm and blues*? I wouldn't. For better or worse, it was pop music, and it was my pop music. The personality of those artists influenced my thinking, my feelings, and, later, my actions the way only pop stars can influence young people. I'm not sure if there's anyone who influenced me more.

Pop stars are somehow simultaneously accessible and archetypal: they are casually authentic, mythologically powerful, and the coolest friends you've got. Pop stars tend to embody the value system and worldview of teenagers but with the bodies of gorgeous young adults, because they usually are gorgeous young adults. Pop stars of the nineties danced a lot, and in intricately choreographed numbers. I, too, loved to dance.

There is a Polaroid of me at four years old wearing a Bartman T-shirt and no pants, holding a karaoke microphone. I have a very sweet little smile that curls up on the left side with the tiniest hint of self-consciousness that my picture is being taken. My mother says I started saying around this time, "I want to be a singer on a dancer stage." There are dim but deeply rooted memories I have of dancing exuberantly at a wedding at the same age, sliding on my knees across the wooden dance floor. My mother tells it like I impressed everyone at the wedding (where I was a ring bearer for my nanny of two years), and that I refused to dance with anyone—my face was screwed up in a preternatural stinkface and I was dead serious about cutting a rug in my tuxedo with tails.

It was always a cuteish story I could appreciate as I got older because music was, and has always remained, my inspiration, my rock, my happy place. Harder for me to appreciate, though, was how real that little boy's yearning was. He didn't only want to listen—he needed to move. He had his eye on a North Star whose guiding light was *play* and *expression*. He was connected to his body in a way that was totally alien to me at twelve. (If you haven't read my other essays yet TL;DR: I spent a lot of time alone.) There was little dancing of any kind from about six years old onward, and by the time I moved to Los Angeles, I had been chubby for years. I hated my body.

When I listened to music, that self-consciousness melted away. When I watched music videos, however, I was met with beauty standards for men and women that were absolutely fucking insane, and which I accepted with a slow, terrified nod of my head.

Yes. I believe that's exactly what my babygirl and I are going to look like.

I was given more instruction in relationships by Sisqó, Ginuwine, Usher, and their countless peers than either of my parents. In that world—the pop star matrix—the arc of an entire relationship never needs more than three minutes for sufficient exploration, and that's with a fair amount of repetition. Infidelity is a standard, so no love is ever safe, and yet love conquers all and lasts forever. There is the important addendum that often the best kind of love lasts for just one night, because it feels like forever. Whatever, I know this will make sense when I'm older.

What is clear: when pop stars sing about love, they mean sex. Since I know nothing about sex, nor how to cultivate love in a romantic relationship, my conflation of the two will become increasingly complicated and inextricable over the next several years. By the time I'm in a relationship and having sex, it will be too late. The pursuit of happiness, for me, consummates and ends in a vagina, the very place I came from, and that symmetry is the closest thing I have to a relationship with the Divine or any other raison d'être.

My pop star associates emphatically agree. *He is learning well.* I can see them nodding their heads, and some of them even wink, if they aren't wearing sunglasses inside. Theirs is a wordless and jubilant confirmation building toward an epic climax that releases in a screaming falsetto riff with their hands outstretched in fingerless leather gloves. It isn't possible to be hyperbolic about the import of a falsetto riff as I am coming of age. For the lovesick protagonist who emits such a sacred and salacious cry—and make no mistake, he is sick—he nears closer to his beloved with every breathy intonation. Closer to being enough. To being loved. There is no peace for him. The only relief he has from his condition is to modulate the key and go higher.

Remember when I said I put headphones on and I'm gone? We've only just left the airport, and I don't know what anyone is complaining about with the traffic here. I would gladly sit in this yellow cab all night listening to the Dru Hill catalog (including singles and remixes), taking in the lights and sights of the city as we roll through it at seven miles per hour.

My mother and I arrive in Hollywood nearing midnight at the Motel 6 on Whitley Avenue and Hollywood Boulevard, a few blocks east of the complex which, in the next two years, will begin hosting the Academy Awards. The LA of 1999 is seedier than the Oscars would have you believe. On the corner is a Western Union where my mother intermittently sends and receives money wires. Across the street is *the* Frederick's of Hollywood, suggesting there are more elsewhere. In the display window is an array of voluptuous mannequins, all flaming-hot, headless women. Averting my eyes feels like an empty promise, and made to whom? Nonetheless, I do try. I'm trying a lot of things. I live in LA now.

This is what I've told my classmates in Tacoma, at least. To be clear, my mother and I haven't yet moved full-time to Los Angeles. Our sojourn to a salty street corner in the center of Hollywood is only a weeklong test run to see if we can do this—"this" meaning leaving our home and my father in a quasirural suburb in Washington State for Hollywood, California. Here, I will audition for movies and be in them and never go home. This will become my home.

Decades later, long after having achieved this goal, moving to LA will strike me as pure delusion given the statistical improbability of making it, but for my mother and me at the turn of the millennium, it seems like a fruitful endeavor. It doesn't seem crazy. We're not crazy people. Something is driving us out of our home to chase a dream. The truth is, our little family of three is falling apart and anywhere other than home seems better. This fact, coupled with another—that I love performing and that what I care most about is being an artist—seals our fate as a family. Four months transpire between this first beta trip and our final move to Los Angeles. I can only recall a few moments from this intervening period, when I was back in Washington State awaiting my family's decision regarding the permanent move to Los Angeles.

First, a conversation with an eighth grader who could not believe that I, a seventh grader, made out with two girls in a hot tub. It happened by the end of my first week in LA! My exclamation now is one of disbelief, not pride. As a grown man, it's hard to recall what the intermediate bases are between first and home when referencing degrees of physical intimacy, and I'd rather not try to remember or clarify them. We did go past first base—and seriously, God bless us, these three children making poor choices together. My memory—I'm cringing, not in a funny way—is that they were half sisters. I hope they were stepsisters, and that my memory is off. Either way, this eighth grader back home in Washington couldn't believe it, and his heart was in the right place.

My only other memory from this brief time back in the Pacific Northwest is performing the monologue from *Hamlet* in front of my entire seventh grade in the theater/lunchroom. Nearing the end of the school year, the opportunity to make declarations about your growth and potential were there if you wanted to make them. Apparently, I did. I wouldn't even finish the school year before leaving, so this was me dropping the mic and dipping in dramatic fashion—quite bold for such a shy boy, and exactly why you should watch out for the quiet ones. Shortly after I nailed this monologue, we headed south for palm trees and sun. The last image I have of my home in Washington is driving away from it in our Ford Taurus hatchback, my father standing in the rearview mirror with my dog sitting at his feet as I held back tears.

One of the first things I start doing in LA is going to drop-in hip hop dance classes on Lankershim Boulevard. Hollywood is a different kind of place. It's got some toxic environments and people who populate them, but it is very hard to find a boy who won't at least try to dance. I'm going to the Millennium Dance Complex (which everyone refers to simply as Millennium, a killer name in 1999) where pros and amateurs comfortably mix, and a few teachers are blowing up choreographing for Britney Spears and NSYNC at their peaks. Some of these classes are huge, and they are all very intimidating, but I'm inspired. I belong to a fringe demographic of shy white boys trying to become actors who have been told dancing would be good for them. Within that demo, I'm an outlier in that I already know it's good for me. It's great for me. It's my literal dream, and I didn't even have to ask for it. Is this what people do here?

I'm thirteen now, I've been attending classes for a few months, and the young women and men who turn up to Millennium on a daily basis to devour these dance routines appear to me exactly like they've come from the pop star matrix. Some of them have—like, they *are* the people in the music videos. Each class generally ranges from students who are sixteen to twenty-four years old who are ripped, hot, and very talented. I'm short and chubby, and my terrible fear that I won't grow up to be like them compels me to believe that I will absolutely grow up to be like them, tilling the soil for seeds of self-loathing that I'm not conscious of yet.

November. The month of my birth and the release of Sisqó's solo debut *Unleash the Dragon*. There was much else going on, like Y2K and the outset of my life's work. In August I'd booked my first acting gig on *Will & Grace*, a huge show at the time. For anyone who has just moved to Hollywood, this is a dazzling triumph, a glorious first. Many never get this far, and not this quickly, but it's only a detail, if I'm honest about my priorities at the time.

Far more consequential to me was a brilliantly sunny Sunday afternoon when my favorite hip hop teacher, Jason, showed up with Sisqó's new CD. I saw it flash as he popped it in the stereo system, and I froze. Time slowed. Which track would he choose? The album wasn't yet the cultural event it would become, but I'd already had it on nonstop rotation. The only single released from the record so far was "Got to Get It," with a music video directed by Hype Williams. The next single, as yet unknown, was surely not due for a couple months. There were so many potential hits, and no one could know which song Sisqó would choose as his sophomore single to cement the legacy of his solo debut. No one knew that, in February of the year 2000—when the future would become the present—Sisqó's next single would eclipse every song of Dru Hill's that came before it and overshadow anything he would release later.

Jason cues up the track, but no one can see the face of the hi-fi stereo receiver. No sound emits just yet from the giant speakers suspended from the ceiling of Millennium's converted warehouse space with wooden floors worn smooth by thousands upon thousands of dance routines. Moments before the reveal, it's still Jason's secret, a pause I think he must enjoy a little bit every class. I'm waiting, actually holding my breath, when I hear the sampled *hiss-pop* of a vinyl record and now I know the song. Now I know that here, within the mirrored walls of Millennium's largest studio, I am part of a vanguard. There is a feeling of prophecy—we are humble disciples who will, in time, spread the gospel, but first we must learn from our teacher. Our sequence of intricate choreography will be to Sisqó's "Thong Song," and I know that I will leave everything on the dance floor today.

I glance around me to see who else recognizes the song. Some do. Some don't. Like time, the track keeps going with or without us, so I find a spot on the floor to call my own for the next hour as the staccato strings begin to pulsate. It's as though I'm hearing "Thong Song" for the first time. Something is dawning. There is a monumental journey ahead. I imagine this is how astronauts feel during a countdown, or how Harry Potter felt when he discovered he was magic. The mission is great.

"This thing right here . . . ?" Sisqó asks rhetorically over the strings. He's not singing yet because he needs to us to prepare. No one will be the same, and he knows this. The measured rise of his intonation is that of a master. What is it? What is *this thing*?

"Heh—"

Sisqó offers us the first syllable of what would be for plebes *haha*, but withholds the last. His restraint reveals the ordinary haphazardness of mortals, who mumble and bumble or trail off and gaze at their navels. Now a lead violin offers an aching top-line melody, a sighing lamentation.

"Is lettin' all the ladies know . . ."

He pauses. In his silence, behind the microphone, I can perceive a single Sisqónian eyebrow rising minutely.

". . . what guys talk about."

The way his mouth curls around the *ow* sound in "about" gives the impression that he is withholding a secret, or a tongue ring. He holds some knowledge, some eternal truth that would cause the multitudes to become enraged and engorged. To keep them sane and relatively docile, he knows he's got to get on with it:

"You know, the finer things in life."

And upon the utterance of what word but "life" do we hear the first shaker, the first lean on the straight classical rhythm thus far introduced. It's two quarter notes that start between the one and the two, then four sixteenth notes between the three and the four (I think, don't quote me). It's the sound of a peacock's feathers unfurling before he swoops in on your girl. It's a knowing wink, an indication of what's going to happen on this dance floor, and so Sisqó laughs a throaty laugh, ad-libbing just before the one:

"Check it out—"

Like so many who try to recount what it's like inside a flow state, Sisqó can't tell us anything more about what he's doing; he can only do it. The verse begins, and the rest of my time in class will be like catching a behemoth wave that will test the limits of my capacity until I ride it to its resolution on shore. Only then will I be able to look back and realize what I've accomplished.

The steps of the routine Jason conceived are long forgotten, but the feeling of doing the damn thing is still there. I also recall what I was wearing—black Airwalks with khaki cargo pants and a red sleeveless Old Navy shirt that was my go-to no matter the weather, no matter that the sleeve holes opened to reveal my chunky body (more than I realized, thanks, blind spots!). I had a middle part in my longish hair, and I felt sexy. I felt vindicated. I felt relief from the bizarre cultural norm to not dance when you hear music; to not laugh joyfully as often as you can; to generally not express yourself; to not say wholeheartedly to someone that you do love them; to not love yourself. Clearly, I was starting to adopt the traits of masculinity that seem like healthy armor to a boy but become something far closer to a prison. Dancing was a way to shed this armor I could barely perceive I'd begun wearing.

But that is all in retrospect with (some) maturity and (almost no) wisdom speaking. In the moment, it was an adrenaline rush of hormones. Puberty was nigh. My sex drive wasn't fully engaged yet, but thanks to the music I listened to, and the career I was pursuing, I was ready to become a gorgeous sex icon. The engine had begun revving on that plump little body of mine for a while and I was ready to break out the gates. The way I moved on that Sunday afternoon was a love letter to those I could not yet know and the numberless lovers whom I would never know. I entered something of an altered state, though there was no demon or illness in me—only a yearning that couldn't find its highest expression in coitus. So, in sublimation of such a force, I was subject to tectonic gyrations. These feelings came from on high, or down low, or perhaps from the window to the wall. Whatever the source, I was an instrument.

The feelings *were* this powerful, and there was some evidence in Jason's response at the end of class. He would usually select someone to dance alone as a demonstration for the rest, to say, "This is how it's done." The people he chose were always incredible. That's how I remember it, at least. Surely he must have chosen some more for their spirit than their technical prowess, but all I can recall are phenomenal performers. So, as we're nearing the end of the dance number, I'm really feeling myself and I hear a commotion, but I'm barely aware of what it is. I finish, and realize Jason has been making a scene, getting people to back away and give me space. I can't make out what he's saying over the music—if it had been 2024, it would have been "Let. Him. Cook."—but he is beckoning me to the center of the floor, indicating that I have been chosen. Jason cues the track up one final time.

There isn't a moment for me to think, or to shy away from the portal yawning open before me. I will perform in front of the class by myself, which also means this will be the last time I'll ever dance like this to Sisqó's "Thong Song." Where else could the opportunity possibly arise? It won't. This is the beginning, middle, and end of a fantasy becoming a reality, a fleeting moment I will cherish for the rest of my life.

I killed it. I don't know, maybe I didn't. I know I haven't danced quite like that before or since. By the time it was over, the class was clapping and cheering and I immediately knit myself back up. I didn't let myself smile. It was uncomfortable to accept this praise, or to believe that it was authentic. It should have made me happy, because I wanted not only to be picked, but my God, I wanted to dance. I wanted to do this dance over and over for the rest of my life if it would feel like this. But when it happened, I denied myself the joy of having it the moment it was over. Walking a few short steps to my mother—yes, a little weird but fine, my mom was there sitting and watching the whole thing, like a handful of moms did every class—I acted like she and I had to go. There was nothing for me to gather except a hoodie. I took my time with that hoodie.

It's the zipper.

My mom said something encouraging like, "Honey, they're clapping for you." I ignored her. Her claim still feels like a dubious one, nearly twenty-five years later.

In the following weeks, my tap teacher offhandedly referred to me as "Jason's little protégé," which remains the only empirical proof that all of this did happen and that people other than my mother saw it. I'm sure my tap teacher wouldn't have recalled saying this even a few days later, but it was a morsel of validation in the wilderness of rejection and judgment that characterized most adolescent social spaces and, even greater, Hollywood. Nowhere else was I getting that kind of overwhelmingly positive feedback.

Dance had medicine in it for me, and I had something to offer as a dancer.

Taking anything seriously can be difficult for a teenage boy, never mind the things that make you feel free—and vulnerable. I was acting, yes, but dancing as well? *Chill.* By my fourteenth birthday, only a year later, I'd stopped dancing at Millennium, or dancing at all, except when legitimized by the presence of girls. What dancing looked like from that point on until my midtwenties was mostly grinding. I ground with force and vigor, and when that fell out of style, I just didn't dance much.

Years later, living in Williamsburg, Brooklyn, I realized that I still had a habit of trying to grind when all these chic nerds preferred something that seemed comparatively wholesome. They danced in large groups to bands like Bon Jovi and Hall & Oates with big, goofy smiles on their faces. They knew all the lyrics to this music, and I swore I was hearing much of it for the first time. *Is this how adults dance?* I wondered. Sisqó did not prepare me for this—nor Ginuwine, nor Usher. I had to learn how to restrain myself in these situations and, somewhat paradoxically, to open up. In a grind, one tends to have a singular focus and a facial expression marked by determination. Just dancing with friends, on the other hand, I was seeing a lot of raised eyebrows and pointing fingers and laughing (these were their dance moves, to be clear—they weren't pointing and laughing at me). At first, this sort of dancing bothered me, if not bored me a little bit. While not as viscerally stimulating as the ass-to-crotch mating simulation prevalent in my teens, this had an ease that felt liberating. As a former dancer, I would sometimes question myself: Why didn't I know how to dance freely anymore?

To be clear, I did not eat, pray, love in a dance circle and regain access to my inner child while "Virtual Insanity" by Jamiroquai played one night in a sweaty club. I'm an adult. Change happens very slowly. There is, almost surely, no song that can change my life anymore, and not because I'm closed off to the possibility. I am simply now older than most writers and performers of pop music, and because I'm still aging, pop songs have less and less to offer me. That is, unless I'm on TikTok.

No, hear me out. Listen. On TikTok, a pop song can adopt new life and meaning because it's deconstructed and repurposed by the children of the world!

My first foray into TikTok was late summer of 2019. I barely dipped a toe, and the ripple effect was comparatively huge—something I could not have foreseen at all due to my deeply ingrained millennial biases against new social media.

At the time, a close friend of mine who goes by the name Kris Yute had just released a single of his music and I wondered if I could support it somehow.* A simple repost on Instagram or Twitter would do next to nothing (y'all never click through and you know it), so I knew it had to be a video, and I knew it needed to organically reflect our friendship. If it did that, the song might get boosted a little.

At this point, Kris and I were about twenty-three and thirty-three, respectively, two (mostly) grown men peering into the foreign landscape of hyper-media-savvy teenagers. Kris showed me a little dance that one of his grassroots fans had created for his song just after its release. It's a very simple set of moves that involves your arms, mostly. I don't know that anybody has or will ever successfully

---

* The song is called "I Did It." Look it up, if you so desire.

describe a TikTok dance in the pages of a book, so I won't try here. The short of the long is that we did the dance, and it was terrible. Those first takes were so cringey and unusable that it could ruin my career. We were standing up, and you could see too much of my tiny two-bedroom apartment that no one would believe I lived in then. Absolutely nothing about it worked. It wasn't what the streets wanted to see.

Despite being a millennial through and through, I knew the key was to stop trying, so we simplified it: we sat down. Nothing says you don't care like sitting down for a dance. We each put our own spin on the super-simple routine—for me it was a hard pop of the neck, which would later polarize people in the comments—and I posted it on Instagram. It ended up on TikTok (a place I believed I would never go) and there it took on a life of its own. If this is the first you're hearing about it, I understand how hard it is to appreciate, but this video of ours was a cultural moment. That's facts. Everybody (surely not everybody) knew Kris Yute's song and our little dance on TikTok by December of that year. The Gen Zs—let me speak for them—loved it. It became such a popular trend that Dr. Phil chose to do it for his first post when he started his account. The joke was that, if he was going to get on TikTok as a curmudgeonly old man, he knew had to do this dance to win over the kids who run the app.

Did I receive far too much credit and praise, like many celebrities do when they cosplay normal? Absolutely. But like my tap teacher hyping me up over twenty years prior, it was a moment of validation for my desire to play—in particular, to dance.

Then the pandemic happened. TikTok blew up even more. I still had no interest in joining whatsoever, but I saw my stepson—in his first year of middle school on lockdown—become rapt in front of the smartphone my mother-in-law got him for his birthday (without telling us initially, thanks, Ma). He started dancing in his bedroom all the time. I'd never seen him enjoy dancing like that before. Uninterested in the platform as I may have been, I understood then the import and relevance TikTok had for its users. I didn't dismiss it, but I still felt it was not my medium.

Fast-forward to October of 2022. *Podcrushed* had premiered that spring, and my cohosts Nava and Sophie were becoming very media savvy. They knew one of the keys to our gaining an audience would be finding them on social media, so we started a TikTok account for *Podcrushed* and we all got the chance to experiment. The obvious question (for Nava and Sophie) became: When is Penn going to get on TikTok? Over that summer they applied what should be recorded for posterity as a healthy pressure, and then, in October, Taylor Swift released her album *Midnights*.

Taylor Swift is to adult Nava what Sisqó was to little Penn, and just like little Penn knew before the masses that "Thong Song" would be a massive cultural moment, Nava knew that Taylor Swift's "Anti-Hero" would be a massive cultural moment. They are not the same, nor equal, but there is at least this one connection. (I am curious if there are any others between "Thong Song" and "Anti-Hero.")

This was a potentially prime moment for me to enter the chat and start my TikTok account, because this highly meme-able clip from Taylor's video—answering the door to find the evil version of yourself—worked very well with the Penn Badgley–hates–Joe Goldberg narrative. Briefly, I have been publicly critical of my own characters ever since I started being interviewed (whenever that was) because I don't see anything wrong with it. I can watch a show and throw popcorn at the screen just like anyone else (people do throw popcorn at the screen still, right?). In my *Gossip Girl* days circa 2007, my judgments of my own show didn't exactly win hearts and change minds. Even though it was all very Dan Humphrey, the early aughts weren't a time for meta-engagement in the press. I was young and perceived as inexperienced, possibly ungrateful, especially when my comments were denuded of their context and intent.

Fine. Twelve years later, when *You* hit Netflix, the culture had finally caught up to my vision. With explicit social commentary baked into the show's premise, a critical approach to my character Joe Goldberg worked very well—it may have even been needed.

So, we shot the "Anti-Hero" TikTok. In it, I run through Sophie's apartment toward the door like I'm in a terrible thriller, wearing the same gray pants and black shirt that I'm wearing in probably 80 percent of my TikToks because I am nothing if not a basic bitch. I throw a desperate and chaotic look over my shoulder before I open the door to find who but—Penn Badgley in a *Podcrushed* hat! Is he Joe Goldberg? For copyright reasons, there's no reason anyone should assume it's Joe Goldberg. I literally didn't say a thing about him.

Now, as a man entering his late thirties, one who takes his craft as an artist seriously—however unserious I may be—my nervous system was on fire with resistance to making my first post on a personal TikTok account. I hated it so much, and so predictably, that Sophie knew to record the moment and make a TikTok out of it (what a social-influencing snake eating its own tail *that* is). The most important distinction to make, though, is that I had fun while we made the video: I got to perform a little, direct a little, and be absurd. Lip-syncing and chaos are two of my most hidden talents, or they were. Anyway, this post was another cultural moment. There were news items on CNN about my arrival to TikTok. I will bite my tongue and overlook my darkest concerns regarding what that says about our culture because my original North Star of *play and expression* was guiding me, which was even recognized in The Comments.

I hesitate to mention The Comments at all because they will see this and come after me. The comments section of any social media platform is generally a place where conversation, reciprocity, and goodwill go to be maimed and eviscerated like Jim Caviezel in *The Passion of the Christ*. But to my genuine surprise, the comments on my TikToks were full of appreciation and gratitude for a little boost of serotonin. Art Blakey—acclaimed jazz drummer and a serious artist if there ever was one—once said something to the effect of, "Anyone can write a sad song. It takes a genius to write something happy." The point I infer is that a work of art that brings joy without sacrificing complexity, depth, or nuance is a work of the highest genius. This, I believe, is why my TikToks are not genius. But at least they bring joy.

You may have noted: *You didn't do any dancing in the "Anti-Hero" TikTok, though, breh.*

No, because I'm not a puppet. I knew what the people wanted, so I needed to do it on my own terms and at my own pace. I had waited ten days, which on TikTok is like three and a half years, and Nava was nudging me, ever so kindly, while I assured her that I could take Kendrick-level intervals between hits. And on the eleventh day I dueted a Meghan Trainor dance—no time to explain what that means, Mom, I'm wrapping up here—and this was my big reveal, the sophomore release that cemented my legacy as either daddy, zaddy, or king. This post garnered more headlines and news items (still very concerned for us all), but I'm going to gloss over this one because it's not where I perceived the surprising heart coded deep in the algorithm, and thus, found my *place tok*.

About two weeks after my much-celebrated antiheroic arrival on the app, the *Podcrushed* team came to visit me in Brooklyn so we could record some in-person episodes of our podcast. They tried to show me a TikTok from one of our listeners, and before I could slap the phone out of Nava's hand, screaming, "We are not changing TikTok; TikTok is changing us!" I saw a face I recognized—a genuine superfan of mine named Lauren who playfully declared she would post herself every day doing this little dance she'd created until I dueted it. For her dance, Lauren chose a sped-up version of "Money Trees" by Kendrick Lamar. Touché, Lauren. She had my attention.

The dance was so incredibly simple, so incredibly short, that I couldn't not do it. Even Sophie (a notoriously terrible dancer) could learn it, and this was helpful because the *Podcrushed* team had to do it together. Lauren had done it with a handful of her friends behind her like hype men, and I love relegating Sophie and Nava to hype men. What you see in this TikTok is eight people total on split screen (four on Team *Podcrushed*, four on Team Lauren) rocking our clenched fists back and forth at waist level as our hips rock back and forth in the opposite direction.* It's a very small movement but, I must say, with eight people moving in unison, it has a hypnotizing swag (I must also say that a chess match with

---

* Remember when I said I wouldn't try to describe a TikTok dance? Repeat after me: "We are not changing TikTok. TikTok is changing us."

"Money Trees" playing over it would have swag, to be fair). What I love about it is that it represents an unlikely truth in our era: the most pure and wholesome effort can, sometimes, be the most rewarded. As of this writing, although the matter of copyrights has left the Kendrick song muted, rendering our dance tone-deaf and nearly irrelevant, it is still my most-watched TikTok at over fifty million views, nearly twenty million more than my other most-viewed posts. This number only matters because of the spirit behind it—I was shown some love, and all I had to do to reciprocate was rock with the beat for a few moments with a few of my friends.

When I imagine myself dancing, there is a meridian in my body that I want to activate and expand: it starts in my chest and radiates out into my arms. I can feel it now. I want to reach my arms out in opposing directions as far as I'm able while arching my back and sticking my chest out (and maybe my tongue). Then, I want to bend my legs to connect that line stretching across my chest to a vertical meridian, a line through my torso, into my pelvis, down my legs, and out through my feet into the earth. I want to do it barefoot on clay with warm, fresh air and sunlight bathing me. Clubs can be great—I don't know, can they be great anymore?—but it's only one form of dance, and one environment. It requires the veil of nighttime and, for most people, alcohol. Why aren't there more ways we dance?

If you can talk, you can sing.
If you can walk, you can dance.

This is an old proverb from Zimbabwe that I first heard at thirteen or fourteen years old in the gorgeous introduction of a

Reflection Eternal song rapped by Talib Kweli. I don't know how it's possible that, at least in America, we find ourselves so rarely in spaces that welcome song and dance. All children do it. When does it stop for us? Why? I mean to ask in a manner that isn't rhetorical. Maybe you're able to ask yourself and discern a real answer. There are reasons we stop singing and dancing, and I know for me it was a convergence of many factors which, if I trace the tendrils of each root, unite eventually in a single cause: sadness. The question that must follow, then, is what caused this sadness? The simplest and deepest answer I can think of is *disconnection*—from others, and from myself. One informs the other, and I'm not sure which came first, exactly, but I know it was a very long time ago.

I don't dance nearly enough to claim that, through movement, I've reconnected severed parts within myself or established some great bond with, say, my cohosts (#foreversevered). I don't even feel comfortable saying, "I dance." Self-consciousness persists, but my North Star has reemerged. I'm interested in seeing where it will lead me if I have the courage to follow it.

HAIR

SOPHIE

I stepped into the salon, timid and tentative, my nervous breathing masked by the whirr of blow-dryers and chatter. At eleven years old, a salon birthday party was the epitome of sophisticated and cool—two things I was not. The rest of the girls gathered for this party had grown up together here in the Philippines, and, relatively speaking, I was a newcomer.

On the day of Lucia's party, I had been in Manila for almost three years. My father's work with UNICEF had our family moving from country to country every two to five years, and the Philippines was the sixth country I had lived in by the time I was eight years old. Although three years was an eternity relative to the timeline of my life, I had spent the first two years with a different crowd. My regular crew of friends was more low-key than Lucia's, and the two groups didn't exactly mix. While I was flattered to get the invitation to the party, I wasn't totally sure why it had come my way. I *had* picked up on some hints at school: a compliment on my shoe choice here, a request to sit next to each other in class there, but an opportunity to hang out outside of school was something new. The girls at this party were decidedly more popular than me and my friends, so the fact that they plucked me from obscurity gave me butterflies. This was my chance to prove myself to them.

Lucia had handpicked a dozen friends to come and get their hair done at a trendy salon followed by a ladies' lunch at Max Brenner. If you were in middle school in the mid-aughts, you know what a big deal Max Brenner was. Picture the undeniably sleeker, trendier, older cousin to a TGI Fridays, where everything on the menu involved chocolate—even the salad. A tween girl's *dreamland*.

I had a budding friendship forming with Lucia and most of the girls at the birthday party, but I was still a little unsure of my place in the group. They had a foundation of closeness that was impenetrable. All of their parents mingled regularly at dinner parties, events, and on vacation. To varying degrees, each of the girls' families were part of Manila's "elite."

My parents did not travel in the same circles as the rest of these parents. They had other events and social gatherings with fellow expats, but they did not mix with Manila's wealthiest. When I was properly inducted into Lucia's friend group, I got to peek into a world that looked like it was lifted right from a magazine. My mom would pick me up from a playdate and I'd gush. I'd hop into our minivan, and before the door was fully shut, my mom was already pressing me for the details. "What does it look like in there?!" she'd ask with a twinkle in her eye.

Behind tall gates and security outposts were courtyards with reflecting pools, lanais* with fancier furniture than my living room, decked-out pool houses and Kelly Wearstler–level design. Very quickly, this new world behind its tall garden walls made my perfectly good life seem like not enough.

The wealthiest families in Manila often had a fleet of household staff: maids, cooks, drivers, gardeners, pool guys, sometimes bodyguards, and often a nanny—called a *yaya*—for each child.

Standing in the pickup line at the end of the school day, you'd see *yaya*s leap from tinted black Suburbans with cool washcloths in hand, ready to wipe sweat from the brows of the children they looked after. My family did not have a black Suburban with tinted windows, and no driver, either. I hung around campus for more than two hours after school most days because my mom refused to do more than one school pickup. She would roll around at five o'clock in our silver Nissan minivan, no washcloth in sight. So, not only had Lucia and co. known one another since the womb, but their *families* ran in the same circles; they had for generations. Beyond their family ties, there was a shared social strata they inhabited that was beyond my reach, rendering me an outsider no matter how many birthday parties I got invited to.

One by one the girls were whisked away by stylists who guided them across the gleaming marble floor to chairs waiting for them. The girls took their seats down the line, and aprons went flying in a domino effect before landing wrapped around their necks. I was the last one standing. My eyes flitted about, wondering where *my* stylist was. I caught the eyes of Lucia's mom across the salon. She

---

* A lanai is a covered outdoor space, common in tropical climates where it is warm year-round.

was looking at me but her arms were crossed, and she was leaning to the side, quietly conferring with the last available stylist. Before I had time to wonder what they were saying, they made their way to me. Lucia's mom stood beside me and lay her hands gently on my shoulders. She crouched down to tell me that my hairstyle would be ". . . different" from the rest, as if the closer she got and the quieter she spoke, the softer it would land.

Aside from me, all the girls at the party had straight hair. Still, each one was getting a blowout. Even though they were essentially straightening their already straight hair, something about a blowout screamed, *"I am elegant. I am classy. I am an adult."* Because my mom rarely let me use heat on my hair, I had been waiting weeks to feel glamorous at this party, just like the rest of the girls.

The stylist ran her fingers through my curly hair as I winced. My mom's words rang in my ears: *"Never brush your curls."* The stylist took a clump of my hair in her hands, held it above my head, and let it fall a few strands at a time. I could see her face in the mirror, and she was looking over me in disapproval. "We won't be able to blow-dry your hair," she told me. "We'll do something else."

I glanced over at the rest of my friends, each of them with a blow-dryer and a round brush at their heads. I watched their hair fall from the brush like the shampoo commercials I'd seen on TV: smooth, shiny, and thick. Pantene in real life. I knew that my hair wasn't straight, but I had certainly blow-dried it before, so I knew for a fact that it was possible.

My face got hot and my palms started to sweat. My sister, Siria, always poked fun at the way my hands got clammy at the slightest bit of nerves. She'd swipe her fingers across my palm and recoil; my brother, Kalan, would pile on. I hated when they ganged up on me, but now I wished they were here. They would have stood up for their little sister. They would have said something to Lucia's mom. Instead, I just sat there while the stylist raked her hands through my curls, leaving them separated and frizzy.

I spent the rest of the time in the hairdresser's chair in a muted state. All the excitement for the day had drained out of me, and I let my mind wander while the stylist tugged at my hair. I couldn't make my hair straight. I couldn't change the fact that I wasn't born in Manila. I couldn't force Lucia's parents to become friends with mine, and I couldn't make my family upper-class. I was getting invited to the parties, but I wasn't going to penetrate. I had been aware of our class difference, but, until now, it seemed like an issue that was reserved for the adults in our lives.

The stylist decided to braid my hair into cornrows that stopped at the crown of my head, where the braids led into the poofy mass of my now-brushed-out curls. She finished each braid with a big, bright, yellow plastic flower clip. I felt like a child at a party where the rest of my classmates were being treated like teens.

This wasn't the first time I'd found myself wishing for the silky, straight hair most of my friends had. Growing up in the Philippines and China, I didn't have many people to look to with curly hair. At school, on TV, in magazines, commercials, and on billboards—everyone sported shiny dark hair. Shortly after moving to Manila, I became obsessed with wigs. I dreamed of running my hands through straight hair without my fingers getting caught in my tangles. At the time, it seemed like nothing more than the quirky fixation of a child, but looking back, I realize I would have done anything to cover up the hair I was given. My mom was the only person I could see myself in. She always assured me how beautiful my hair was, but in this moment she wasn't there. It was just me and the hairdresser. And I knew what *she* thought.

As the appointment came to an end, the girls gathered by the front of the salon, one by one. Lucia's mom touched my hair and stepped back. "Wow! You look like Beyoncé!" she said. I wasn't sure how to respond.

I think I was the last to join the group, although I can't say for sure. It's like when you think someone is taller than they are just because of their personality . . . I don't know whether I was actually apart from the group, or if that's simply how it seemed to me, because I felt so much like an outsider. I wonder now if Lucia's mom noticed the way the whole experience made me feel. Why didn't she step in when she saw me being othered?

Maybe she realized what I see now—I was just a fleeting member. While the rest of the girls had deep roots in the Philippines and would probably raise their own children there, I was a visitor. This was the sixth country I had lived in, and because of the nature of Dad's job, I could only stay a maximum of five years. I came late, and I would be leaving early. Lucia's mom didn't know my mom like she knew the rest of the parents; she wasn't going to be seeing my folks at any social gatherings. If she had noticed that I was upset, she wasn't going to have to face anyone about it, so it didn't really matter.

Once everyone had gathered by the salon entrance, we walked across the outdoor mall to make it to our reservation at Max Brenner. We squeezed into a large, round table booth, a gaggle of girls with bouncing blowouts . . . and me. I don't remember what we talked about, who exactly was there, or what I ate for lunch. What I do remember is how badly I wanted to claw those dumb yellow clips from my hair. I dissociated for the rest of the afternoon.

I don't know if Lucia and Bea and Grace and Mari and all the rest of the girls had any idea that our worlds were so different. In my mind, there was a gulf between us that I had spent all my energy trying to bridge. Did they notice the details like I did, or were they too focused on their side to even notice mine?

I didn't spend much time thinking about my racial identity as a kid. My mom is proud of her heritage, but in raising us, she felt strongly that it wasn't something that should define us. She grew up in the UK, where race as an identity is not quite as defining as, let's say, nationality or class. She is half Black, making me a quarter, which has left me feeling like I'm not quite mixed enough to claim it. My dad is white, with an Anglo-Saxon mom and an Ashkenazi Jewish father. I am in the liminal space between white and Black, and there are times when that part of my identity fades into the background. But every so often something happens that brings my racial makeup to the fore.

Why wouldn't the stylist blow-dry my hair? Why did she braid it instead? Why did she use those god-awful kiddy clips? And more important, why did it make me feel so small?

No one wants to feel othered. Ever. But especially not when you're eleven and you're hell-bent on fitting in.

Even though we didn't talk about it much in my household, I did grow up feeling proud of my Blackness. My mother's father, Earl Cameron, was one of the first Black actors in the UK to break the color bar in the fifties. In 1951, my grandfather starred in a film called *Pool of London*, where he played a character who was involved in the first interracial romance in British cinema. There's a story that my mom told throughout our childhood of how when money was tight and he could have used the check, he turned down a part in a film that portrayed Black men in an undignified way. He took every opportunity he was given to uphold the nobility of human beings, especially people of color.

As an adult I've come to feel more and more connected to my Blackness. Today I would love having cornrows. Screw a blowout. But Lucia's birthday was the first time I would experience the dissonance that came to characterize my experience of race as a mixed person over the next couple of decades.

When I came to the US for college, I was pushed to define myself by my race more often. Questions of "Where are you from?," "What are you?," or "Why don't you speak Spanish?" had me stumbling to figure out what information people were really looking for while giving me some insight into how they viewed me.

I wonder what my relationship to my racial makeup would be if I had chosen to go to university in the UK instead of the US. My grandparents married in the UK before the Supreme Court case *Loving v. Virginia* made interracial marriage legal in the US. In 1967, the year of *Loving v. Virginia*, 3 percent of marriages in the US were interracial. In 2015 that number rose to 17 percent.[*] Nearly ten years later there is research to show that the percentage has grown even more. As the world becomes more globalized, I suspect being mixed will become more of a norm and fewer mixed people will feel the pressure to identify with one group. But as a

---

[*] Statistics taken from the Pew Research Center report on "Trends and patterns in intermarriage."

kid born in the nineties, I still struggle with confusion over where I fit in.

At thirty, I find myself reliving the salon debacle of 2005 over and over again. I haven't had cornrows since I was about fourteen, and I never went to another salon birthday again, but the feeling of being different—and more specifically, of not being enough—persists. I'm not white enough. I'm not Black enough. I'm not smart enough. I'm not wealthy enough. I'm not successful enough. I'm not edgy enough. I'm not cool enough. I'm not sure enough. Thankfully, these feelings are getting quieter the older I get, but I'm becoming comfortable with the idea that they will always be there in some capacity.

I've tried to pinpoint where this feeling of inadequacy began, and eleven years old is the closest I've gotten. I don't blame Lucia, or her mom, or any of the girls at the party for not noticing what was going on internally for me, because I didn't quite understand it myself. But knowing how deeply these experiences as a tween in Manila affected me makes me conscious of the intricate, delicate, and complex inner world of any eleven-year-old I come across now. As I feel my not-enough-ness slowly wane, I imagine eleven-year-old Sophie taking out those obnoxious, plastic, yellow hair clips one by one, and it feels magnificent.

I WASN'T MEANT FOR THE NFL

NAVA

I'm at my friend's wedding, and it's hot. Phoenix-in-the-summer kind of hot. I'm in my thirties and I'm wearing a backless dress... for the first time.

You might be thinking... *So?*

But I assure you, this is a capital *B* capital *D* Big Deal.

Let's rewind three decades.

. . .

My older sister, Zhena, and I both attend the Episcopal Cathedral School (ECS) in San Juan, Puerto Rico. We moved from California to Puerto Rico with our parents in 1988. Zhena is having a harder time than me but we're both struggling. Neither of us fits in, exactly. In addition to the fact that we don't speak Spanish as well as the other kids, we're culturally different. Zhena and I are half American, half Persian. Our Persian mom makes our food*

---

* See "A Family Recipe" for more on this topic.

and dresses us. Mercifully, our school has a uniform. But about eight times a year, there are casual days where kids can pay a small fee to dress in normal clothing. Casual days are special events at ECS. The kids go *all* out.

While my classmates were often in cute jeans and tops adorned with the face of the Disney princess du jour, I was always dressed more like an *actual* Disney princess—frilly dresses and embroidered tights. My mom wanted my sister and me to look like "little ladies," and her version of that was, apparently, Little Bo Peep.

In addition to not looking or sounding the part, we were also Bahá'ís. Because if being another ethnicity doesn't single you out enough, a minority religion hardly anyone has heard of on a deeply Christian island is there to seal the deal.

In the adolescent fantasy version of my life, all of this otherness is erased by my undeniable beauty. *Who cares if she's different? She's so hot.*

But no, I don't have that going for me, either.

Beauty is subjective, but certain cultural standards dominate our definitions of beauty, largely dictating taste, and I met none of those nineties standards in Puerto Rico.

Big boobs? Mine barely register.

Small nose? I'm a Persian girl who never got a nose job. It's just science, folks.

Tiny waist? Within reach, if I had been more willing to rigorously diet.

Big butt? (Absolutely a thing in Puerto Rico!) Just a modest one, my friends.

I did have, I think, lovely, long legs. But at the time, nobody really talked about legs. It was all boobs-butt-waist. All my friends talked about it. Sometimes we took turns measuring one another's waists. (I often slipped out of the room right before it was my turn, too mortified for anyone to find out mine was twenty-seven inches,[*] because, yes, I'd already measured at home.)

By seventh grade, in spite of some obvious body image issues, I'm doing a much better job of fitting in. My Spanish is pretty great. My friends all accept my religion and have heard enough about it to not think it's weird. I'm dressing myself (I have embraced denim), and I'm doing my best to blend in. So far, I've only had one big crush, in kindergarten. I'm probably due for another.

Enter Diego.

We're not zoned by neighborhood, so none of my classmates live close by. None except the new kid, Diego. We're actually within walking distance of each other. When we realize this a few weeks into the school year, he starts coming over to my place so we can do homework together. As we get closer, he begins asking me questions about Camila, my pretty best friend, whom he's developing a crush on. As handsome Diego inquires about beautiful Camila, I develop an ardent crush on him. He's vulnerable. He's cute. His hair! His arms!

This crush lasts all the way through senior year of high school, but it is one that I will never acknowledge—even when Diego finally asks me directly if I like him in the tenth grade. When I evade an answer, he laughs, *"Come oooooonnnn!"* (Subtext: I already know! Just admit it!) I can't remember how I replied to this, but I know I lied. I was so convinced there was no way he felt the way I did that I didn't even consider simply turning the tables, asking him if

---

[*] What I wouldn't give for a twenty-seven-inch waist today!

he had a crush on *me*. (Even now, the thought that he might have confronted me about my feelings because he wanted me to like him feels both obvious and impossible.)

Alas, Diego and I never have our *they will* in the will-they-won't-they scenario I play out for six years in my head, but we do have six years of true friendship. Because of Diego, I am the only girl allowed into the inner circle of a group of boys that includes Mateo—brilliant, hilarious, will grow up to bear a striking resemblance to Orlando Bloom and date half of my best friends*; Santiago—cartoonist, atheist,† perhaps the edgiest member of the group; and, of course, Diego—heartthrob, athlete, human golden retriever.

Roughly twice a week we do homework together, go swimming at the pool or beach by my house, and compete for the funny crown, trying our best to outdo one another in the insults department. We are the kinds of friends where the more brutal the dig, the more beloved you are by the group. But no amount of thick skin could protect you from the things said *earnestly*, not meant to cut deep.

Like when I'm a little too honest with Diego about how Camila, *his* crush, perceives him as not driven enough for her. (She would go on to change her mind, and the two would engage in a prolonged

---

* Everyone will accuse us of being secretly in love with one another well into our twenties, and we will disappoint them all with our boring, platonic friendship.

† I'm Bahá'í, and Santiago and Mateo liked to poke fun at how into my religion I was. Once they declared they'd started their own religion: Phoha'i. Exactly like the Bahá'í Faith, but with a strange and urgent emphasis on photosynthesis. Did I mention we were not the coolest kids in school? (Except Diego, who definitely was one of the coolest kids in school!)

back-and-forth of never liking each other at the same time, but liking each other frequently and intensely whenever one of them did.)

Or when Mateo calls me and says, "This morning Mom said she thought you were the prettiest girl at prom last night!"

"Really?" I was so excited. I was sometimes considered the smartest girl in class. I was voted friendliest for our high school yearbook. But no one had ever accused me of being the prettiest.

"I mean, you looked really good! But the prettiest girl there?" He cracked up. Too ridiculous an idea to even contemplate. (This didn't cut *too* deeply because there were so many gorgeous girls in my class that I never aimed for prettiest. But it did sting. Enough for me to remember twenty years later, right?)

Or the time Diego and I are standing next to each other in the kitchen, drying off after a long afternoon by the pool. I still remember which swimsuit I'm wearing. A tie-dyed two-piece, green and blue, with a halter top, my entire back exposed. A swimsuit I'd picked out with my mom—the open back a compromise because the bottoms were little shorts and it covered most of my stomach. My mother is reasonably conservative. She doesn't let me show as much skin as most of the other girls in my class are allowed, but she does let me show way more skin than most of my non-school Persian friends are allowed.* Until that moment, it's my favorite piece, picked out for special occasions.

Diego looks at me. My heart pounding. Finally, he speaks.

"You should be a linebacker," he says.

---

* In a fun turn of events, as I got older and she got nervous about my lack of experience, she sometimes encouraged me to wear tighter clothing.

I barely follow sports, but I know this is a position in football.

"What?" I smile tentatively. *Is this flirting?*

"You know, because your back is so broad."

He raises his shoulders twice and extends his hands out, to indicate *broad*. He smiles at me sincerely and then bounds into my living room to hang with Mateo.

"Mateoooo!" he calls out cheerfully as he goes.

I stand motionless, crushed.

For months I've been wondering if he likes me. If he thinks I'm cute. But now I know. *He'll never like me and my stupid, broad back.*

I stand for a moment in total silence before the tears rush down my hot, red cheeks. I need to escape. I walk past the boys in the living room, concealing my head in my towel, pretending to dry pool water off my face, and then rush into my bedroom, where I close the door and cry.

My big, broad back racks in sobs.

I wish I could just brush it off. Not take it to mean more than it meant—a comment offered carelessly by a boy who saw me as a friend. The kind of friend he could say anything to, including *you should be a linebacker*. He isn't trying to cut me down a notch; he also isn't trying to date me.

I become convinced that it's because I don't look like the other girls in my class. Where many of my classmates are curvy and petite, I'm tall and big-boned. I feel all wrong. I don't fit in with my friends in Puerto Rico, but I also don't match the girls on my TV. The first time I see a character I can *remotely* connect with is Keri Russell in *Felicity*. Felicity is a soft-spoken, intelligent young woman who uproots her entire life because the boy she'd been pining over all of high school wrote her a sweet yearbook message. I related to her because she was the first lead actress I'd seen on a teen show with curly hair, and the first who was deliberately smart. Keri was also rail thin with big green eyes, so the physical similarities ended at the curly hair. But I clung to what I could.*

I have middle school diaries full of self-loathing messages, like "If I weren't so ugly, maybe Diego would like me instead of Camila."

"Hey, little heifer, stop eating Oreos, or no one will ever want you," a funnily cruel one reads (pretty sure I had just seen *Clueless* and Cher refers to herself as a heifer after eating a handful of candy).

When I look back at old photos of myself, I was so cute! Not girl-on-TV cute, but cute nonetheless. Unfortunately, I wasn't the only one absorbing media messages about women's beauty. The boys were, too. Diego was, too.

Hot girls have small frames. Big boobs. Tiny waists.

That was the message—ubiquitous, relentless, punishing.

I would listen to my friends size up the girls they liked. Their best features. Features unlike mine. I would even chime in at times. Smiling on the outside, withering on the inside.

The summer I turned sixteen, I got down to a size 2 (0 at the Gap!) by eating a thousand calories a day. I kept it off for exactly one year and then gained it all back. But that summer, ten boys, several of them extremely attractive, asked me out or let me know

---

* Also, can we acknowledge how absurd it is that producers cast someone as stunning as Keri Russell to play an invisible bookworm—a notion Scott Speedman addressed in an interview once, where he pointed out it felt ludicrous to play a guy who wasn't instantly smitten with Keri.

they had a crush on me—eight more boys than had ever liked me up to that point.*

That summer I internalized the message that there's nothing more attractive than being thin. It's a message I have tried hard to unlearn. *But*. If I'm being honest, I don't think I've ever fully forgiven myself for not being able to get that skinny again. I'm constantly aware of my weight and my size, and my confidence in dating seems to be in direct proportion to the inches around my waist.

That said, when I watch shows now, a smart lead with curly hair is nothing to write home about. I have seen, with true awe and wonder, women represented as desirable and hot who I could never have dreamed of seeing onscreen even as a sidekick when I was a teenager. I'm so thankful that younger women have a much wider array of protagonists to see themselves reflected in. Sometimes I feel jealous. I wish I would have seen them, too, when the core messaging in my brain was being wired.

Still. I also wonder how the constant exposure to more traditional notions of "hotness" on social media, for instance, is impacting our young people. Last year I had to make a pact with myself: I'm not allowed to look at a certain female celebrity's Instagram page.† Every time I do, I feel awful. I wonder how our twelve-year-olds are faring with this 24/7 access.

I wonder how twelve-year-old Nava would have fared.

That thought sends a little shiver up my spine.

---

* There's a whole other essay I could write about the tragedy of not being allowed to date until I was in college.

† A beautiful woman around my age, who loves posting herself in swimwear.

And speaking of twelve-year-old Nava, there's a question we ask all our guests on *Podcrushed*: "If you had a chance, what would you say to your twelve-year-old self?" I've had three years to think about this question, so forgive me if I'm long-winded.

If I had the chance, and if she had the capacity to hear me, here's what I wish I could say to my twelve-year-old self:

Don't waste time on boys who don't like you because you'll miss out on the ones who do.

Protect your heart.

Don't protect your ego.

Watch less TV; it's making you hate yourself.

Be silly with your friends.

Cherish your family.

Get a dog.

Dip your body in the ocean every chance you get.

Don't worry about the swimsuit!

Lie under the stars and eat s'mores by the fire.

Don't feel guilty about the s'mores!

Seriously, get a dog.

Learn a cheesy song on guitar and play it in front of your crush.

(Preferably a dachshund.)

Dance your little heart out.

Don't let a boy who doesn't care, or a cruel inner narrative, rob you of the sweetness of your life.

This is the only one you get.

. . .

It's 107 degrees in Phoenix. I'm hot, I'm sweaty, but I can't stop smiling. Two of my favorite people are getting married today, and my very attractive ex-situationship has just sidled up next to me, placing his hand on the small of my back. He whispers, "I really like your dress."

I suppress a giggle, feeling exuberant. I'm not a linebacker in the NFL. I'm just a young woman in the prime of life, curly hair blowing in the wind, feeling the sun on my skin and the breeze on my broad, bare back.

MAX BECKER: CERTIFIED HOTTIE

SOPHIE

"Have you seen the new kid yet?" Bea asked under her breath so Mr. Carson wouldn't hear.

Our math teacher was roaming the room, making sure we were focused on our independent work. I waited until he passed my desk to respond. "Not yet, but I've heard he's tall."

"Tall, tan, and blond!" Bea replied with some rhythm in her voice.

My eyes, wide, darted over to her.

At the beginning of every year there is an influx of new students at any given international school. But this was different. Max Becker was joining us a few weeks into the start of eighth grade, when the general hum from the start of school had died down. His timing was impeccable.

The International School of Manila had students from all over the globe. But the vast majority of my classmates were from Asia. When you looked over the student body, you might see two specks of blond in a sea of brown and black, but no more. Max was . . .

exotic, and his arrival had the whole grade talking. *A blond new kid? In our grade? And he was cute?* The eighth graders must have done something special in a collective past life to deserve such a bounty.

The rest of math class was a wash. Once Bea put Max in my head, there was no hope for anything else to make its way in.

In the cafeteria at lunch there was more chatter among the girls about this mystery Max. I had yet to see him in the flesh. To me, he was both mysterious and mythical. That is, until I walked into French class with Monsieur Robert.

I had been caught up chatting with my friends in the hallway and was characteristically late to class. By the time I arrived, there was only one open seat, and it was next to the not-so-mythical, very real, very hot Max Becker. My heart started pounding. I scanned the room for another open seat, any seat! I was unprepared. I had daydreamed about many boys before, filling several pages of various notebooks with "Mrs. [insert crush's last name here]" scribbled all over. As my doodles might suggest, my experience with boys up until this point had been flirty and fun, but mostly fantasy. Max seemed mature, and I had not had a "mature" romantic experience yet. I knew the stress of sitting next to a cute boy was not worth the story I would be able to tell my friends.

While I stood frozen between the door and the desks, deliberating, my classmates had all turned to look at me. My eyes met Max's. They were blue. *Of course they were blue.*

I flashed a sheepish smile at him before lowering my gaze and pulling out the chair next to his. Bea had undersold him. He had golden-brown skin and shaggy hair that had been bleached platinum by the sun. In all the murmurings I had heard today,

I picked up on the fact that Max had arrived a few weeks late to school because he was on a surfing trip in Thailand with his family. *A sun-kissed, golden beach babe by my side.* The heavens were shining down on me.

I barely looked at Max for the rest of French class, but I felt his proximity to me. If I moved my forearm a few inches, our hands would touch. If my knee rotated a few degrees, our bodies would meet. My entire being was buzzing. *Comment dit-on, électrique?*

Monsieur Robert gave us our homework assignment for next week, and textbooks started slamming shut around the room. In the shuffle of the end of class, with my head down in my planner, I felt Max turn to me. "Hey," he started, "I'm Max." His voice was low and steady.

My eyes slowly raised to meet his for the second time that day. "Sophie," I chirped with a subtle wave.

A smirk came across his face. He knew the effect he had. He was standing now, and the fluorescent lights overhead created a halo around him from my vantage point.

"See ya 'round, Sophie." He swung his backpack over one shoulder and left the room.

I did some quick mental math (making up for what I had missed in Mr. Carson's class). I thought of the most sought-after eighth grade girls that Max could go for. Grace, Melanie, Esther. Grace was basically married to Jack; I could cross her off. Even though they were rocky, Melanie was technically still with Enrique. Another one down! And Esther had sworn off boys after the fiasco with Jonathan at the end of last year.

With Grace, Melanie, and Esther off the roster . . . I might actually have a shot. Possibilities swirled in my head. *Would our kids* be brunette or blond? Would they get my nose? The hint of German in his accent?

There was just one, tiny, complicating factor: my parents. Helen and Dale were staunchly against dating. Unfortunately for them, they were raising a daughter whose MSN Messenger password was boycrazy94. They were at a loss for how to manage my fervency. I sometimes wondered if their views on boyfriends and girlfriends in school was the very reason for my obsession, but neither of my siblings were as determined as I was to experience romance, so it was hard to blame my parents.

Every time I broached the subject of dating, my dad would repeat the same refrain, "You'll be allowed to date when you're married."

"Haha, very funny," I would grumble.

I had had "boyfriends" in secret before. But it was innocent stuff. We'd exchange a coy wave in the hallway, our friends would giggle, and that would be enough to sustain us for months. So even though we called each other boyfriend and girlfriend, I didn't feel like I was disobeying my parents. What's in a name, anyway?

The weeks rolled on and Max and I started to build up a flirty rapport. Our knees eventually touched under the desk in French class. He searched for me until we locked eyes through our crowd of friends at lunch. He found reasons to walk me to class. I was starting to take the hint. When a mutual friend told me, "Max wants to meet you by his locker after school," one day in October, I had a gut feeling I knew what it was about.

A giddiness steadily rose within me. Throughout the day word spread to all our friends. The excitement was palpable. When the bell rang, I started to make my way to the fourth-floor hallway to meet Max; with each floor that I climbed, the posse of girlfriends grew around me. I rounded the corner on the fourth floor and found Max, with his own posse of our guy friends behind *him*.

I don't know if I blacked out or if he didn't even have to say anything because we all knew what this rendezvous was about, but I have zero memory of the following three minutes. All I know is that I must have said yes to becoming his girlfriend because he pulled me in for a peck on the lips to seal the deal. We had our backpacks on, which made it hard for him to execute his moves as smoothly as he intended; we both knew that it was the next step in a prewritten script, but it was awkward and clunky.

While Max was perfectly sweet, the kiss felt perfunctory. Nevertheless, our friends erupted in a cheer. I walked away from that block of lockers, officially Max Becker's girlfriend.

I should have been on cloud nine. My friends certainly were. But now that I was living it, I just felt queasy. I wasn't allowed to date, and this was decidedly different from my exchanges with "boyfriends" in the past. I had been comfortable with some cheeky secrecy, but this was a new level of duplicity and it seemed to crack something inside me. It felt wrong to blatantly disregard my parents like this.

I avoided Max the next day at school. I made it through the day by peeking around corners and ducking behind trash cans. He texted me that night.

Max: i didn't see u at school today. were u sick? i missed u.
Sophie: nah, it was just a busy day. missed u too.

Maybe this would all go away on its own? Best-case scenario: it would fizzle and I wouldn't have to say a thing.

The following day was similar, more peeking and ducking. Thank God Max's cute blond head was so easy to spot from a distance. *This isn't so bad*, I thought. *Maybe I could keep this up till January?* It seemed to be working until after lunch when I opened my locker and a note tumbled out:

> y r u ignoring me?
> —Max

I was going to have to deal with this after all. The thought of telling Max the truth mortified me.

All my friends were allowed to date, so telling him I wasn't would make me sound like a baby. My parents were noticeably stricter than the others. They concerned themselves with my whereabouts, what I was up to, and who I was with. One evening when a friend pushed me to sneak out to McDonald's with her, I came up with all sorts of excuses for why I couldn't: "It's late," "I'm tired," "It's cold out," "They'd catch me," etc. All those things were true, but the real reason was that rebellion for rebellion's sake didn't appeal to me. It never occurred to me to sneak away from my safe, warm nest in exchange for . . . what? Stress, some social capital, and a small fries? No thank you. There would be plenty of times in future years when I *did* rebel, but the reward of McDonald's and some thrill didn't entice me enough to step out-of-bounds at thirteen. The guardrails my parents set for me matched the ones I set for myself at that age.

While I complained to my friends that my parents were overbearing, I privately welcomed their involvement in my life. I can recall multiple sleepovers and hangs with friends when I begged my mom to make up some excuse for why she had to pick me up early, just so I could pretend in front of my friends that I was bummed I couldn't hang for longer. While my friends were sneaking out, I was sneaking home.

At times, the double act was exhausting and hard to keep track of. Pretty much everything in my life as a teen was telling me to listen to my peers over my parents, but I had a hard time following suit. I loved my parents. I felt safe with them. I trusted them and I often wanted to return to them. But it would be social suicide to admit that to Max or any of my other friends in eighth grade.

Up until now I had kept a safe distance between home and school, family and friends. But I was starting to feel the effects of splitting myself in two. My true self was standing in one spot, feet firmly planted on the ground, and a shadow self—a translucent version of me that wanted to please my friends—was floating further and further away.

Once I saw Max's note, I knew my days of burying my head in the sand were over. I had to be honest with him. I enlisted a friend to tell him to come to our meeting spot (his locker), alone, after school. I had a plan to tell him the truth. To tell him that even though he was kind and caring and a certifiable hottie, I couldn't continue to defy my parents.

Max bounded over. I opened my mouth, but instead of what I intended to say, a flimsy excuse came out.

"We . . . can't be together," I blurted. "I just don't think it would be wise to get attached, you know, since I'll be moving in January, and . . ." I could feel myself overexplaining. *Keep it simple, stupid Sophie.* I fidgeted with the bottom of my school uniform shirt and trailed off. Max didn't press me.

"Friends?" He opened his arms for a hug. I breathed a sigh of relief. As always, he was the perfect gentleman.

I'm grateful to Max for letting me off the hook. It's not easy facing any kind of rejection. Maybe he sensed the relief it brought me to knit my split selves back together again.

Eventually, I did feel comfortable pushing my parents' boundaries around dating. After all, is it not the duty of the youngest child to buck against the established rule of law? I took that responsibility seriously! At the end of tenth grade I would start dating my high school boyfriend, even though my parents' rules had not changed. My mom and dad tried to stand their ground, but they could see that there was no stopping me. I was going full steam ahead into the world of high school relationships.

Why was it that just two short years after I crumbled in front of Max Becker, I was so confidently going against what my parents wanted? Standing in front of Max, at thirteen years old, I was not ready to date. Maybe the splitting of selves that I felt wasn't so much the effect of going against my parents' wishes as it was going against mine. Two years in teen world is like two lifetimes, and I had done enough growing in that time to feel comfortable following my own timeline. My parents' rules had served as an essential protection against the peer pressure that was coming at me from all sides. And in the time I spent inside that bubble of safety, I built up my own fortress. It was constructed on the foundation of my parents' wise counsel, but over the years I fortified it with the brick and mortar of my own values and experiences.

In adulthood, I've wondered about the weight I continue to place on my parents' opinions. At thirty years old, is it appropriate to seek approval from them as much as I do? I can concede that sometimes it breaks the bounds of what might be considered healthy. When I was twenty-four and the thought of telling my mother I got a tattoo sent shivers down my spine, I knew I might be too reliant on her approval. I ended up breaking the news over the phone a few months after the fact, and I'll never forget her response. After a minute of thick silence, in an uncharacteristically slow and gravelly voice, she said, "I can't help but think this is symptomatic of something deeper." *Ouch.* Knife sufficiently twisted. I spiraled.

I've flip-flopped over the years, trying to decide how productive it is to care so much about what they think. For now, I've settled into a nice middle ground: in a world that puts so much emphasis on individualism, it's important to have people in your life whose opinions you value, whom you can trust to give you feedback that keeps the various parts of you attached to your core morals. I am blessed to have found that kind of trust in the two people who gave me life, so I seek their advice whenever I can. The part of me that would sneak home to my parents in search of their counsel and approval as a teenager is still very much there.

As a teen, my parents taught me that my own inner compass needed to be strong enough that the opinions and actions of my peers shouldn't dictate mine. As an adult, I'm learning when this advice applies to my parents as well. It's taken a lot of practice and patience to shed the habit of seeking my parents' blessing for even the inconsequential things. I asked my mom what she thought of the new painting in my home, and when she said she didn't love it, I started creating a listing for it on Facebook Marketplace. I talked myself off the ledge, though, which is progress.

Even though my relationship with Max lasted seventy-two hours, forty-eight of which I hid from him, I'll always be grateful that he didn't hold anything against me. When he could have pinned me for leading him on or messing with his emotions, he saw my true intentions instead. A certified hottie *and* a nice guy? Here's to hoping someone has snatched him up by now.

ON A WEDNESDAY

NAVA

Growing up, everyone knew I hated Wednesdays. My girlfriends would call to make plans and stop mid-sentence: "Oh, it's on Wednesday, though." I dreaded Wednesdays all week long, glorying when they ended, trembling when they rolled around, inevitably, after every Tuesday. It all goes back to a decision my parents made in 1988.

In the spring of 1988, on the very day Farahnaz and Tommy Kavelin closed escrow on their first home together in San Fernando Valley, California, Tommy received a letter in the mail. It was a list of states with new openings for translators in the US federal court system.

"Farahnaz," he called my mom over. "There's an opening in San Juan, Puerto Rico." As a Spanish-speaking US territory, Puerto Rico has a federal court. Tommy (American) and Farahnaz (Iranian) both happened to speak Spanish. They also both happened to practice the Bahá'í Faith,* and dreamed of being pioneers. In the Bahá'í Faith, pioneering refers to the spiritual act of leaving one's home—often relocating to another city, country, or region, to help the local Bahá'í community grow—and to contribute to the advancement of society through spiritual and social education. My parents had pursued a few pioneering opportunities before, but my dad's highly specialized training as an interpreter in the United States federal court system greatly limited their options. This felt like the perfect opportunity, especially because they had also heard that the Bahá'í community in Puerto Rico was in need of pioneers.

Farahnaz walked over and looked at the list with her own eyes. When her gaze fell on San Juan, Puerto Rico, she looked up at Tommy and without hesitation proclaimed, "Let's go!"†

A few months later, at the age of three, I was on the shores of San Juan with my dad, my mom, and my six-year-old sister, Zhena. Needless to say, my upbringing was "religious," and while that word holds negative connotations for many, I cherish my Bahá'í upbringing. Among other things, it meant that my family

---

* The Bahá'í Faith is the youngest of the major world religions, founded in nineteenth-century Persia by Baha'u'llah, whose title means "Glory of God." Bahá'ís believe Baha'u'llah fulfills the ancient religious prophecies of a Great Redeemer who would come to establish peace on Earth. The Bahá'í writings provide a framework for drawing on science and religion as complementary knowledge systems to build a peaceful and unified world. Bahá'ís around the world are actively engaged in educational, socioeconomic, and discourse efforts to improve the conditions of their local, national, and international communities. Bahá'ís are encouraged to use consultation to make decisions of all kinds, at every level of society, based on the premise that the search for truth demands differing perspectives.

† My dad's eyes well with tears every time he recounts this story, and he tells me he fell more deeply in love with her that day.

and I spent a majority of our free time engaging in acts of service together. Our home was completely free of substances* and their often-destabilizing influence, and we turned to consultation both as a tool to make important decisions (with my sister and me each getting a vote!), and as an instrument to resolve difficulties. We also actively nurtured bonds of community with our fellow Baháʼís and had a real sense that there were friends, and even institutions, we could rely on in times of duress.

Prayer was also a constant in our home and in my life. As a baby, my parents put me to sleep by singing prayers to me every night. By three, I was memorizing prayers I could say if I wanted God to "guide me, protect me, illumine the lamp of my heart." I don't think I've had a single day of my life go by that didn't include the recitation of at least one prayer. I rely on it as I do water—for nourishment and survival.

Until about the age of twenty-two, though, I complied with the Baháʼí laws of prayer out of a sense of duty, but I wouldn't say I *looked forward* to praying. I mostly rushed through my daily devotionals, distracted by everything else in the world, including the curtains, the carpet, where my other shoe might be.

When someone turned to a longer prayer at a meeting, I would try not to visibly cringe. Zhena and I would sneak a glance at each other when an elderly gentleman in our community would start lightly chanting one of the longest prayers in the book (a solid ten-minute chant on a good night). We would try not to laugh, as we knew the other was thinking: *The Tablet of Ahmad* again?!

---

* Any mind-altering substances, e.g., drugs and alcohol, are prohibited in the Baháʼí Faith.

Sometimes when my parents caught us, they would glare at us; other times they would try not to crack, too. Once, inexplicably, the four of us got so simultaneously hysterical (what we call a *pavera* in Puerto Rico), we each had to leave the room, one by one.

I have so many memories of lying in bed with Mama as she stroked my arms and chanted prayers to help me fall asleep. Of Dad excitedly reading a passage from whichever new sacred text he was currently studying. As a family, every time we got in the car,[*] we each took a turn sharing a short, powerful Arabic incantation for protection—a prayer that has saved my life more than once.

As a family we served together. We opened our home to a constant stream of Bahá'í visitors who came to Puerto Rico. Stranger or friend, if they needed a place to stay, our home was open. (Zhena and I often had to give up our bedrooms for these visitors, so we weren't always thrilled to receive them.) We visited sick members of the community. We spent time with the elderly. For most of my youth, we weren't allowed to take a family vacation that didn't include a service component.

My mother's favorite way to serve was to open our home for a devotional gathering, where anyone of any belief or background could pray together. But she wasn't contented with simply opening our doors for prayer. She had to offer a feast—at least three different Persian meals, along with appetizers and desserts—and the feast had to be offered in a home that was immaculate. While she prepared the lavish meals, Zhena and I were expected to clean. She picked Thursdays as the day of the weekly devotional and in

---

[*] To this day, I can't get in a vehicle without silently reciting it.

twenty years she only cancelled twice—once after she had a heart attack, and once after my dad nearly died.

Since Thursday was Devotional Day, Wednesday became the dreaded Wednesday Night Deep Clean.

While Mom cooked, Zhena and I were expected to clean. We both *loathed* washing dishes and would alternate by week. My moods were particularly volatile on dishwashing weeks. Mom and I were guaranteed to fight. We sometimes got into yelling matches when I tried to skip a Wednesday night cleaning session to hang out with friends. "I have a *life*, Mom!" I would scream at her.

"This is my fault for raising someone so selfish!" she would cry.[*] On and on we went until inevitably I stayed home cleaning, fuming, throwing darts at my mom's eyes anytime she crossed my path.

I'm pretty sure my stomachaches[†] flared up suspiciously more often on Wednesdays. I conveniently planned study groups on Wednesday nights. I locked myself in my room reading books under the covers, pretending I couldn't hear my mom calling out to let me know that it was time to start cleaning. When *Dawson's Creek* premiered on Wednesday evenings, it was a real crisis for me. Historically, I was not allowed to watch TV until I got all my chores done, and I never got my chores done before ten p.m. on Wednesdays because of the aforementioned shenanigans.

Although I tried to scheme my way out of manual labor as often as possible, I *loved* learning about my religion. I happily attended all of our extracurricular Bahá'í educational programs,

---

[*] Persian guilt tactics. Epic.

[†] I had frequent bouts of stomach pain throughout my childhood and youth, until one day they just stopped.

often voluntarily skipping out on a vacation with friends in favor of winter and summer camps where I could learn more about Bahá'í history.

I cherished the stories of young people like Anis and Mona who risked everything to champion the cause of justice. I cried when I read that they were executed and met their deaths with courage and joy. I was invigorated by Tahirih, who tore off her veil to proclaim the emancipation of women. I marveled at the story of Zaynab, a seventeen-year-old girl who disguised herself as a man and defended her community in the Battle of Zanjan, where she lost her life. My heart melted at the endless examples of 'Abdu'l-Baha's tenderness. My spirit soared when I contemplated Baha'u'llah's beauty.

The teachings on the twofold moral purpose (developing our inner talents and virtues *by* serving the world around us, starting in our own schools and neighborhoods) imbued me with a sense of purpose. Faith was not about solitary beliefs practiced quietly at home. It was about transforming oneself to *be* in the world—to interact with it and transform it into a more just and joyful place.

My personal faith and community of practice did not shield me from moments of sorrow and grief, depression and anxiety. There's no way around suffering; it's part of the pattern of life. But my love for Baha'u'llah was an anchor that protected me when the winds of depression or insecurity, bitterness or anger threatened to sweep me out into the sea of self. Prayer and reliance on God, having friends with strong spiritual values to advise me, and parents who were ready to consult helped me move through those episodes. And while I sometimes struggled with negative emotions, hopelessness was rarely one of them. Even in my lowest ebbs, I believed God was real. He was faithful. He was helping me. I also believed that I was capable of change. That life was about movement and growth. There was always a path forward, and a lesson to glean from a difficult experience.

Still, growing up, I struggled intensely with feeling like I belonged. My religion was different. My language was different. My food was different. I cared deeply about the opinions of others and often found myself trying to blend in like a little chameleon, changing my way of dress and the music I listened to depending on who I was with. I was less interested in who the real me was and more interested in who the people around me would accept. I felt more at ease when I was around other Bahá'í youth, though.

Our community was tiny. There were maybe twenty to thirty active Bahá'í youth on the entire island. We adored one another! We understood what it felt like to stand out as the only kid at a party not drinking, not hooking up. We also spent our weekends traveling around the island doing a variety of things that I must fairly characterize as embarrassing.

We established a Bahá'í Youth Workshop, which was essentially a dance troupe made up of several kids who danced incredibly and several kids who could not move. We were too small to be exclusive. Everyone was welcome! Our dances revolved around social themes: Drug use, domestic violence, and eliminating prejudice were the themes I most often danced to. As the youngest member of the workshop—I was twelve and everyone else was about fifteen—I was usually the battered kid. The girl crying in the middle of the stage, surrounded by dancing figures as she lost her friends to drugs. The first kid to put her hand out, crying, "STOP!" when a racist act unfolded.

I wasn't a very good dancer, but I was very dramatic.

Until senior year, I was the only Baháʼí in my grade at school. But I had several Christian friends who shared a similar set of values around alcohol and drug use. People start drinking at a very early age in Puerto Rico, so by the time we were fourteen, this was already a factor at parties. We bonded over being the only sober ones and learned how to be silly without a social lubricant.

Whenever I was at a party where my other friends were getting drunk, three things would happen.

Number 1: Someone would walk up to me and dramatically, tearfully, apologize for drinking, as if it were a personal affront. I never criticized people who drank, and I had no idea why this happened so often.*

Number 2: At least one person, crying, would find me and start pouring their heart out to me, revealing things I'm pretty sure their sober selves would not want me to know.

Number 3: An atheist would confess he† *wished he believed in God. He'd ask me to tell him about my religion, and he'd be completely wrapped up in the conversation. The next day he wouldn't remember a word of it.*

---

* One time in college, I was walking back to my room late at night when a drunk girl I was marginally friends with ran over and flung her arms around me. She started *weeping*, saying, "Nava, I'm so sorry! I'm so sorry I'm drunk. Are you mad at me? Do you hate me? I'm so embarrassed. I'm so sorry!" No matter how much I reassured her that I wasn't upset, she wouldn't stop crying until I gently pried her off me and escaped into my room.

† All the atheists I knew growing up were men.

> *Sometimes, a fourth thing happened: kids would circle around me, chanting, "Drink! Drink! Drink!" and then look alarmed that I might give in.**

When I was fifteen, I started spending summers at Green Acre, a Bahá'í retreat center in Eliot, Maine. For four summers, I studied a series of books about different historical periods of my faith, beginning with a text called *The Dawn-Breakers*. While I learned about the early believers who gave everything to protect a nascent religion from a fanatical clergy and bloodthirsty regime, I found myself growing more confident in my spiritual identity. I was aware of my tendency to hide parts of myself to blend in when it came to my life outside of the Bahá'í community. But if twenty-two-year-old Quddus could be released to an angry mob who tore his body, limb from limb, and tossed the remaining pieces into a fire—all for refusing to renounce his faith—how could I suppress my own? My love for my religious identity, for myself, grew in leaps and bounds.

One of the most special parts of Green Acre was feeling seen and accepted by dozens of other youths. About eighty young people from all over the Northeast, and one little *chica* from Puerto Rico, attended each summer. These were the most Bahá'í youths I'd ever been around. And several of them were *cool*. Objectively cool. The most popular kids at their own schools, regardless of living a "straight-edge" lifestyle. To my own shock, at Green Acre,

---

* I never gave into peer pressure, but I did take a sip of Mike's Hard Lemonade once when I was alone to find out if it tasted as good as all my friends said. It didn't, and I felt awful for betraying my values. That was the first and last time I ever sipped alcohol on purpose.

I was one of the most popular kids. Boys liked me. They wrote me poems. Made me presents. Invested in calling cards to reach me when I got back to Puerto Rico. It felt like entering an alternate universe. At Green Acre, I was happy, confident, and completely myself. But at home, I still struggled to feel at ease.

I went to university in Texas, where I was surrounded by very devoted Christians, who sometimes offered prayers for me not to go to hell. I found that sweet, and not offensive. They cared about me enough to want me in heaven with them, and they took time out of their day to pray for me. I wasn't particularly worried about ending up in hell, either. (At least, not for being a Bahá'í!) But my habit of trying to blend in with those around me reared its head full force when I developed feelings for a Southern Baptist boy who wouldn't entertain thoughts of dating someone outside his faith. I told him I was a Bahá'í almost immediately, but I also accompanied him to church services and Bible studies even though I knew full well I would never convert. I was and will always be a hardcore Bahá'í. I couldn't deny my faith in Baha'u'llah for anyone, not even a green-eyed drawling Southern charmer. But I was suppressing it. While he spoke openly of Bible verses and his love of Christ, I listened and shared little of the respective Bahá'í perspectives. I muzzled myself. I began to feel ashamed over how much time I was spending in Christian spaces simply to impress a boy. I knew it was inauthentic and wrong. There was a self-betrayal in that behavior that deeply troubled me, and when I finally broke free of the infatuation, I vowed that I would never suppress my Bahá'í identity again. For anyone.

My determination to safeguard, and indeed nourish, my Bahá'í identity fresh off allowing it to dim in college, paired with those summers of falling in love with the history of my faith at Green Acre, led to my decision to offer a period of full-time service when I graduated from university instead of entering the workforce immediately. I served at the Bahá'í World Centre, the spiritual and administrative hub of the global Bahá'í community. I committed to two and a half years, but I loved it so much, I stayed for four.

I served as a writer and research assistant for the Secretariat of the Universal House of Justice*—a role I found both strenuous and thrilling. I learned that service could go beyond the physical sweeping of floors or washing of dishes. It could encompass training your mind to solve difficult challenges simply for the betterment of others. Your approach to your career could very well become the embodiment of worship if offered in a spirit of service. Work didn't need to be transactional. Competitive. Cutthroat. It could be collaborative. Oriented toward the collective. Still, I found there was something to physical kinds of service, after all, and against all odds, I began to crave it.

Although I already worked five and a half days a week, without pay, during my fourth and final year, I signed up for an additional evening shift on Wednesday nights at the Pilgrim Reception Centre, where they took care of visitors from around the world who were offering a nine-day pilgrimage.

My job was to wash dishes.

---

* The supreme governing council of the global Bahá'í community.

IN CAMERA

PENN

There are typically three years of middle school in America. For me, there were scarcely two, because I left Washington State before the end of my seventh-grade year. My mother and I drove to Los Angeles in her beat-up burgundy Ford Taurus whose door handles were falling off from the inside and which would break down before we finished the 1,140-mile drive. I choked back a well of tears I barely understood as we pulled out of the driveway and left our lives behind—my father behind—and, like my middle school years, what would have been three became two.

I was twelve. It was a gamble with both my life and my mother's, made by both of us as equitably as any life decision can be between a mother and son, and it wasn't long before our choice was tangibly rewarded. By August of 1999, having left only a few months prior, I booked my first role. It was a big one for a first, especially for a twelve-year-old: five speaking lines on *Will & Grace*, a gigantically successful sitcom at the time. My only scene was with Sean Hayes and Megan Mullally, two masters of the sitcom form in their prime, and I was directed by James Burrows, a legacy TV director and producer in comedy for nearly half of the last century. It was impossible for me to appreciate the far-reaching implications that I was beginning a career.

Despite the staggering odds, after nearly thirty years, the same career that boy started is still going. Whether it is a byproduct or an integral aspect of my career—I'm not always certain which—I have fame, and it comes with privileges and sacrifices that both feel obscene. Fame is an unwieldy and strange power, a unique handicap, a drug, a chimera, an obvious monster, a trickster, a portal, and, among countless other qualities I could list if given the time, it is a mirror. I've come to call it a seven-hundred-pound mirror, one I carry with me everywhere I go, whether I want to or not.

More than a few people (Rob Lowe among them, on our podcast) have called fame a kind of trauma, in the sense that it tends to freeze people at the level of emotional development they had when they acquired fame and began, always unconsciously at first, to live life on its terms rather than their own. If this is true, then it's important to understand where and who I was in the few years leading up to twelve—when I met the seven-hundred-pound mirror for the first time.

When I imagine twelve or later, I see the memory from a perspective in which I am still that person, with so many of the same characteristics, habits of thought, ideas about the world, and artistic desires that I have now. It's much harder to identify with the lonely prepubescent tween who walked the halls of a little private school in Tacoma before he moved to Hollywood, who wore a backpack, had a locker, and went alone to middle school dances with fantasies of impossible romance. That boy had just begun performing in plays as a social outlet and knew the response his nervous system had to the applause of a crowd. He wasn't captivated by any special notion of fame, but understood it as a logical answer to life's problems: a salve for feelings of sadness, isolation, and purposelessness that were emerging as his mind and body developed and his home fell apart.

Memories from this period, which I'll call The Cusp, all take place in the gorgeous gloom of the Pacific Northwest. My parents and I moved from Virginia when I was eight years old to a place called Tiger Mountain on the outskirts of Issaquah, a small town now greatly developed due to the presence of the Microsoft headquarters there. In the mid-nineties, however, Tiger Mountain was approaching the sticks. Our neighbors were a full mile away and our driveway was two dirt tracks carved into mountainous terrain. Three days after our arrival on Tiger Mountain, Wilbur, my sweet little black-and-white cat, disappeared and never returned because the place was teeming with snakes, coyotes, cougars, and bears. It was basically a jungle. I was heartbroken, an only child living in a random cabin in the mountains of a mossy rainforest without a single friend or acquaintance, unenrolled in any school because the summer had just begun. I had only my parents to look to. My mother was racking her brain for a social outlet for me and saw a newspaper ad—a completely relevant medium back then—for community theater auditions in Monroe, a town fifty miles away. I'm sure she was thinking, *We'll be gone all day. Perfect.*

The production was a musical called *The Music Man*, and I auditioned for the role of Winthrop, a very shy boy with a lisp who discovers the joys of creative expression by enlisting in a band, or something like that. If you don't know the premise or plot of *The Music Man*, explaining it will only bore you. The short of the long is that I got the part—the biggest role available for a boy my age—and we began driving a total of one hundred miles to and from rehearsal every day for weeks. On opening night, right after the curtains closed on the final scene, I found my mother just offstage and said, "I want to do this for the rest of my life."

You may be thinking, *Well done, little Penn. You've succeeded. Are we not finished here?*

It's true that the first signs of success came very quickly. Soon I was making regular trips into Seattle to perform with a prestigious children's theater in quirky original plays written by radical progressive teenagers (one feminist piece was titled *The Barbie's Demise*), and my mother and I constantly received feedback that we should try going to Hollywood. That seemed completely outside the realm of possibility then, but it was thrilling to know I was "good enough." Otherwise, I was internalizing toxicity and tension at home. There, I would watch my mother and father viciously fight. They were failing in their marriage—the same enterprise that facilitated my creation. For any child, no matter their age, a divorce is an existential crisis. Thus, this boy who would soon become frozen in the eye of the seven-hundred-pound mirror was contending with existential dread.

I have very few memories of my mother and father sharing closeness. The earliest I can recall was when I was probably ten years old and my parents both in their fifties. We were together for a day trip to the Pacific Science Center in Seattle, which I loved. I sat with my mother and father at a little round metal table flanked with metal chairs in a vast concourse of glass and concrete, light pouring in from giant, vaulted windows on a rare-ish sunny day. We had just bought caramel-covered apples, like silly tourists. Both my mother and father leaned in to bite their apples, but before they could, at the exact same moment, they erupted into a coughing fit which quickly turned to laughter. It was inexplicable to me. They were laughing together, with tears in their eyes, even. I waited silently for a sign of some kind, unsure how to behave as they dabbed their eyes and cleared their throats. Finally, they explained: *it was the powdered sugar*. Of course. They both had inhaled the powdered sugar sprinkled atop the caramel covered apples. And that's it. Moment over. Core memory complete.

I would ask my parents, in the years after their divorce and a safe distance from the numbing pain of their togetherness, "Why did you get married?" My father could only offer a humble chuckle and a shrug, while my mother could say, at least, "I wanted to have a child." Fair enough—she felt she was nearing her biological cutoff—but it is from this place of shaky logic and thorough incompatibility that I came forth (like so, so, so many others). Possibly the highest-stakes feature of childhood is that children don't know how to not take everything that happens at home personally. Children are self-centered (developmentally speaking), so everything that happens between the parents will be, at first, interpreted as a reflection of something the child has done, or who the child is. I remember one evening sitting atop the stairs of the modest A-frame, three-bedroom home we'd moved into after the cabin on Tiger Mountain. I was listening to my parents argue. This argument is only memorable for its crude simplicity. Peering down the stairs to the living room where my parents were just out of view—I'd retreated a few steps back after seeing them march toward each other, shouting in each other's faces—they screamed repeatedly, "Fuck you! Fuck you!" There was a hint of symmetry to the Powdered Sugar Incident because they unintentionally fell into the same rhythm, and so it evolved from a call-and-response to a chant in unison: *Fuck you! Fuck you! Fuck you!*

Hurrah, hurrah.

I was inheriting my parents' misery and anger, and even before puberty, both had new dimension for me. We had gotten a dog, my mother's effort to combat the loneliness and lack of love—a black labrador named Nelly, who had grown into a wild and unruly sweetheart with a lot of personality and no discipline. One afternoon I was alone with Nelly when she wouldn't stop yelping, and my response was to smack her on top of her head and yell, "Shut up, you fucking bitch!" The dog barely flinched or recoiled, just immediately stooped her head as she wagged her tail, already begging for forgiveness and attempting to love me before I'd understood at all what I'd said or done. These had not felt like my own feelings or actions. My mother, unseen from upstairs, called down with a shrill urgency, "Penn! Don't talk to her that way!" After all, I loved this dog dearly. Nelly was a unique solace for me in the tension of our home. She was my best friend. There's a picture of Nelly and me from this same period looking so lovingly into each other's eyes that it's a little weird. I wept with abandon after her death in a way that I was otherwise unable to at eighteen. At eight years old, the only reason I could speak like that to a creature I loved was because I'd heard it before.

By the start of the school year after we'd moved to the mountains, I'd gotten a scholarship to an incredibly small and very odd private school, so well funded that it had a private zoo with sixteen cougars who lounged atop a giant fabricated mountaintop inside of a vast cage. Despite their funding, the school was so poorly attended that, after accelerating through a shoddy fourth- and fifth-grade curriculum, I technically skipped two grades and ended up in a class with no one else in it. This was the first time I would leave school for what my mother called homeschooling, but which was really unschooling. My mother wanted to create ways for me to get out of the house and enrich my life, and hers, too.

Beyond learning fractions with a math textbook at home, my homeschool curriculum—which I can't even say with air quotes—was going to museums in the city, rehearsing for plays, performing for (small) audiences, and, for a brief period, working at a tween-targeted radio station called Kidstar for five dollars an hour (a legal and unionized enterprise). For the time being, all this compensated quite well for the emotional dearth within our family. I was learning from the world and felt like I was an active part of it, engaging in the arts and believing that I could be—I was—a professional artist. Far from a stage parent in this regard, my mother was saving me from the average ennui of suburban youth in America.

Our home was a place that greatly magnified my sensitivities, and while I didn't realize it, I was learning how to protect and harness these sensitivities as a performer and manage those feelings. As a kid accustomed to spending time alone, my experience was mainly through my observations. Thoughts and feelings become something like your siblings when you have none, no constant companion to bear witness to the world alongside you. I watched everything happen around me intently and longed to become a part of it, dreaming of immersion and acceptance in that place. This longing became a powerful charge that, ideally, needed some form of expression. I was a perpetually open circuit, but without a peer to close the loop, I would accept almost any stimulus that might do the job. Books and music became the primary ways for me to connect with the external world, because they were forms of human connection that were always on tap. In fact, people themselves were nearly too much, and the unpredictability of any given interaction was a lot.

I've always been incredibly sensitive to touch. A single fingertip grazing my shoulder blade from a girl at school would be an electrifying event. Anytime, anywhere, for any reason I found myself sitting next to a girl and our legs would touch, even barely, I would freeze and rack my brain while I attempted to parse out what was accidental and what might have been intentional. Foot, ankle, calf, knee, or thigh—the higher the altitude, the closer to input overload. Good gravy on mashed potatoes, I wanted to be touched by a girl. A slap on the back from a jocky popular boy was just as significant and intense, though toward the other end of the spectrum of Attention I Would Like from Other Living People.

Hypersensitivities like this can serve an actor, because you are not the player; you are the instrument. The ideas at the heart of a story are not yours, nor the words you have to say, or the things you have to do. Your sensitivities, then—how you experience the world and respond to it—are your tuning. The alternating harmony and dissonance between who you are and who your character is meant to be produces the inevitable intrigue of a character well played; no one can escape who they are and how they feel. An actor is no different. Being consummately present with who you are and how you feel is, paradoxically, the only way an actor can ever appear to become someone else and approach how they might feel. In this hypersensitive, wholly present state, almost any stimulus is enough to catalyze that change into another. Between "action" and "cut," you become an open circuit waiting for something, or someone, to close the loop.

To me, only one of two things are needed to close the loop and change an actor's state: a stage or a camera. That's it. These two are not the same means, not at all, but both achieve the same end. In the spontaneous and unpredictable real world, sensitivity can feel dangerous, relationships are not glamorous, and the unending continuity of life tricks us so that we often feel like nothing is happening. On a stage, *everything* is happening. Any moment is a scene no matter what you do; doing nothing is often a brave and commanding choice. You are, technically, given the utmost space and time to be and feel exactly as you please, and this is the creative tension in timing.

Of course, at some point you must abide by the structure given you, which is the script—it's the reason you're there, and so with any respect for the material and deference to the form (and the paying audience) you respond intimately at every moment to the plans laid out for you.

This—the play, the scene itself, whatever is written—is the second dimension to the closing of the loop. Your scripted actions and words become your scene partner when you otherwise have none (something I know a lot about). When you do have a scene partner, they are the paramount stimulus. Another human being closes the loop like nothing else can. They can elicit from you something otherwise impossible, because they are another world with another interior entirely unknown to you. There is theoretically infinite possibility between two people. Through this extreme heightening (*drama, my boy!*), the potentiality of human relationships—the stuff of life—can become a little bit clearer to us all.

The stage is often an intoxicating place to be, but I haven't been on a proper stage since I was twelve years old, having moved not to New York City for theater but to Hollywood: the land of film and television. I worked in front of camera by the end of my first summer there, on *Will & Grace*, and I think of this as a soft open.

A sitcom is closer to stage work. The cameras are not at all like the ones used in film or prestige television. They have no depth of field; the image is wide and flat. Three or four cameras operate at once and record from a distance, hovering just beyond the edges of the set like benign and passive spectators. Behind these cameras sits the live audience, who give you what you came for. They laugh, and gasp, and cheer. The only awareness an actor needs of the cameras is to not face away from them. Otherwise, you're on a stage. You must be big and loud even in silence, and you're responding far more to the audience than the mercurial attention of a cinematic camera.

My first true meeting with this latter kind of camera was in my first film role. The movie was called *The Fluffer*. Do you know what a fluffer is? At twelve, I did not. The script was withheld from the boys auditioning for reasons that will become clear, if you don't already get the idea. I thought it must somehow involve dolphins or otherwise cute and cuddly creatures, and this itself was an intriguing mystery because the script pages for the audition contained nothing of the sort—just cinema verité vibes, like any peak 2000s indie film. It was produced by Christine Vachon at Killer Films who had just produced *Boys Don't Cry*, a legendarily intense film with some phenomenal actors and a gut-wrenching story that ended up winning an Academy Award for Hilary Swank. So, this little, elite, vanguard company was making another risqué independent film on a shoestring budget, and I'd landed a role in it. Awesome! Now I had to read the script.

My mother and I picked it up from my agent's office, and I read it before either my agent or my mother did. We only had one copy. In those pages, I soon discovered what a fluffer is, and I explained it to both my mother and my agent as I will for you now. A fluffer is a person who prepares a male porn star for his scene. He needs to have an erection, does he not? A porn production relies quite heavily on that erection, so whatever method is used to arouse him, it's got to be a reliable one. Short of full sex with the fluffer—which somehow seems like having dinner before a three-course meal—the porn star needs something closer to a thrilling and galvanizing appetizer, like a charcuterie board, or a ceviche. So, a fluffer uses their mouth. *That's what a fluffer's job is, Mom.*

Both my mother and my agent were women in their fifties, and both were shocked that they didn't know what a fluffer was, and furthermore, that I had to tell them. Truly, I felt no pressure from either of them as we discussed the merits of the script. Our consensus was that, since I didn't do anything remotely explicit and had some good material to dig into as an actor, it was great.

It was a small but important role, a serious and dramatic turn, and even gayer than *Will & Grace*, if you can believe it. I was playing the titular character—the Fluffer himself—in flashbacks to his first crush, or obsession, as a boy. Rest assured there was no fluffing in these flashbacks. I was doing a lot of watching and waiting, allowed to be an extra-sensitive open circuit, full of feeling, and mostly silent. Possibly most significant of all, I was allowed to express both what the script required and what I actually felt, because they were nearly the same thing. I was allowed to be sad and thoughtful, and if it hasn't become clear by now, I was nothing if not sad and thoughtful at twelve years old.

My character in *The Fluffer* was meant to be from New

Orleans—a sad and thoughtful Southern gay boy—so for my few lines I adopted a subtle accent. The only line I can remember was "What's that cigar taste like?" Emphasis on *cig*. My character, Sean, was meant to be watching his neighbor, a man in his forties, wash his old Cadillac with a cigar in his mouth. Sean was a young photographer, and he wanted to take this man's portrait (not to fluff him—not consciously, at least). Sean was a young artist. He had a darkroom in his basement where he would develop his photographs. That is where most of my scenes were as Sean. And there, in a basement set built on a soundstage, the camera needed to get very close to watch my face where it might capture Sean's growing obsession: the complex feelings of an adolescent yearning for a love more mature than his mind or body are capable of.

I discovered the camera could be an incredible scene partner. It waited like I waited, and it watched as long as I watched. It, too, was an open circuit, waiting for stimulus, recording and responding to every little thing I offered it. Here, acting was a radically different experience than that of the stage or the sitcom set. A live audience necessitates a (great) degree of externalization of what might otherwise be completely internal. On camera for the first time, I was able to dive inward like never before. My audience was only its reflective glass eye.

I had something of beginner's luck on *The Fluffer*, or maybe it was my honeymoon period with The Camera. The television roles I would book throughout my adolescent and teen years set me up for a challenge I didn't expect, that of any working actor: to nurture your love for the work no matter the work you get. Whereas at twelve I was trying to be something of an artist, unmolested by the machinations of the television industry and its metrics, by the time I reached fifteen I wanted to *work*. I needed to work—or it felt like I needed to. I was trying to succeed and make good on the enormous gamble my mother and I had made three years before.

I'd already opted out of formal schooling at thirteen by taking the California High School Proficiency Exam, partly to avoid the on-set tutor experience (one that didn't impress my mother or me very much), but mostly to open up my options in a world of uneducated child actors who were on the path to a multitude of inevitable failures. My goal was to attend college at the normal age as a transfer. This meant I would spend my teenage years taking night classes at a community college, Santa Monica College. There, I would slowly gather the credits (and grades) needed to get into University of Southern California, or somewhere like it.

I did all this—I was accepted to USC at seventeen as a junior transfer—but it was always a tenuous balance with higher stakes than a teenager is typically accustomed to. On one hand, I was lucky enough to answer my life's calling far earlier than most are able to, a gift I've retained and vindicated in adulthood. On the other, what I became focused on as a young actor from the outset was succeeding over learning.

This may be why I still love learning. I never got my fill, neither academically nor creatively. I never attended USC because I was offered a lead in a television series the same fall semester and deferred enrollment for a year (later deferring indefinitely). Two years prior, at fifteen years old, my first lead role in a television series had subsumed my otherwise teenage life with its crushing schedule—twelve to fourteen hours a day on average—forcing me to prioritize time for friends, hobbies, and sleep like a person over twice my age. The closest approximation to anything like *college years* I had were spent at thirteen and fourteen years old in an acting class in a black box theater in North Hollywood.

It was taught by the late Diane Hardin, a woman roughly my mother's age whom I found totally erudite, nurturing, and a bit stern in the exact way a teacher should be. She held the class in a converted retail space that looked wholly unremarkable from the outside. Inside, the space housed two or three tiny black box theaters. Each was a room never meant to be a theater and so, to create the lovely suspension of disbelief needed for an audience, each room was painted black.

A black box. That's the concept. Add a few rows of pitched movie theater seats, a small stage about thigh high, and when the lights are off, you're transported. When they come back on, whether onstage or in the audience, you are in the world of the scene, or you should be. It's so simple and can be utterly mystical with the right performance of the right material, and the beauty of it is that unlike the exorbitantly high-budget production values audiences are accustomed to in film, essentially anyone can do this.

Onstage in those little black rooms, I wept during a performance for the first time. It was an exercise intended to introduce young actors to a methodology for bringing up deep and powerful emotions. Crying was not the clearly spoken goal, but everyone in there knew they wanted to sob on that stage under those hot lights to make everyone else feel something raw (whatever that means). To achieve this was to summit the mountaintop. It was a mythical goal, the training of a monk in the climes of the Himalayas. Could I do it? Could I cry? We were asked to choose a song that had meaning for us, to then sing or speak it onstage, and become so present with the lyrics that the emotions of the song might become our emotions. We would become the channel—not the player, but the instrument.

I chose a song called "Daddy Cry" by the Toasters, a gem of a ska band I'd picked up from one of my skater friends back in Washington State. I didn't like ska at all, but this was a great band. "Daddy Cry" is a song that's almost upbeat (because it is ska), but its tragic theme is haunted by pining horns, and its plaintive lyrics are sung in an understated lilt. It's a wise song, not saccharine or sentimental. I had a preternatural disdain for sweetness and sentimentality already at twelve and thirteen, even more than I had for ska.

To be honest, I barely understood why I'd chosen this song, but I knew it contained something that pulled at a heartstring of mine, so I brought it to class in the black box theater. Onstage, there were stacks of simple wooden cubes, painted black, that we would use for rudimentary approximations of a set—a low wall, or a desk, or a chair. I pushed one of these black boxes just left of center stage and sat on it underneath the spotlights, which had a pleasant warmth to them, especially when nerves made my hands cold and sweaty. They were so bright that they rendered my classmates and my teacher as hazy silhouettes, recessed in shadow—what little audience I had became nameless and faceless for a few minutes. I was given the simulation of being alone as I entered the scene.

"Daddy Cry" was written by a man who has put himself in the shoes of a five-year-old boy who doesn't understand why his father is not there. The boy waits at the door, his nose pressed up against the glass, wondering if it's his fault somehow (remember, children can't help but take the actions of their parents personally). He doesn't like it on his own, and he doesn't know when his daddy is coming home. The boy doesn't speak in the first verse; he waits silently. When the narrator does reveal the boy's feelings, he does it with simplicity and directness. In this way he is holding the boy, caring for him, just as his father would have—or should have—if he had been there.

I began to quake as I neared the end of the first verse, and when the lyrics of the chorus shifted into first person, I became the explicit subject of the song. I was wondering who would tuck me into bed as I prepared for sleep; who would give me a kiss on the forehead as I closed my eyes; who would turn out the lights and close the door to my room. As the song's protagonist, it was me who was listening to the rushing of the wind outside so that I might hear the cries of my father. The shining realization that came to me was that he must have been in as much pain as I was at our separation, and I wept.

As I cried, I found that I was relaxed. I didn't need to prove anything to anyone, not even to myself. My little audience, still veiled from me by the bright hot lights, were audibly listening. Silent. I felt safe in the black box.

Nearly every kid in the class got up there and achieved something of the same feat, and rest assured many of them came from similarly broken or fractured homes. I wonder how Ms. Hardin witnessed it all, the only adult in the room. I hope she knew what a service she was providing, a service far greater than preparation for a career that would elude basically all of us. She must have known we were in peril if we measured our self-worth by our success, if we needed a camera to witness our most vulnerable moments. She let us know, if only implicitly, that we didn't need it.

My best moments as an actor haven't been on camera, or onstage, for that matter. They're scattered across places and times I didn't expect or need it—usually in rehearsals, or the couch of my acting coach in a basement apartment in Greenwich Village where he lived with his wife for over thirty years. John Lennon said of the Beatles that their best songs were never recorded, leaving us to infer that when they would jam onstage or in private, something happened that they were never able to capture satisfactorily. D'Angelo (my personal John Lennon) said years after his 1995 debut album, *Brown Sugar*, that he was disappointed with the recordings, because he believed they had lost the rawness and immediacy of the demos he'd put together with far less money, time, or regard for commercial viability. (This is a well-known phenomenon by musicians, which I've once heard referred to as *demoitis*.) D'Angelo would spend the next five years creating a masterpiece that did capture the electric spontaneity of music that's being discovered as it is being recorded, but it was such an exhaustive work of perfection that one could say he never quite recovered. The attempt to record and preserve any creative process risks destroying it and ruining the results. Physicists (yes, all of them) have proven that observation itself has an influence.

The camera is an especially powerful observer, so its capacity for destruction and ruin is great. It catches everything. You really don't need to do much. In fact, the moment you do too much, it betrays you. It's no better than a middle school crush, really. The less you give it, the more it wants you, and initially this is baffling. Frustrating.

Indeed, like any mean girl, the camera is a complex phenomenon, both in its physical construction and its social impact. The camera's lens—a relatively small curvature of glass between the audience and the scene—manipulates who and what the audience sees, how they see it, when they see it, and even a bit more abstractly, why they're seeing it. This manipulation is the point; it is the great and awful power of the camera. Those who understand this power can learn to perform authentically in front of the camera, but they enter a vicious cycle of sorts, because fame often follows quickly and threatens to contaminate any performance with self-consciousness.

Fame has an enormous impact on an actor's life, on my life, which I'm often unable to ignore anywhere but two places—within the walls of my own home, and in front of the camera. In both places, quite fortuitously, the essence of my role is the same: to be supremely present, and to try at every turn to open myself up, rather than perform what I think would be right, or what I've seen before. This can be difficult in either space, but it is in front of the camera—only in front of the camera, nowhere else—where the seed of fame is generated. The camera is, therefore, the polar opposite of a true home. I have to remember that always: it wears a mask, even while my job is to try to remove my own.

Mid-pandemic, early 2021: I'm filming the third season of my very popular, very beloved, very, very great Netflix series *You*, in which there are quite a few intimacy scenes, as we call them in the biz—simulated sex, or anything sexual like, say, masturbation (my show has plenty of both, for reference). We're shooting a fantasy sequence and as a stylistic choice, one that makes a lot of sense, the director has chosen to place the camera directly in front of my face. My character is meant to be humpin' on his wife, with whom he has become not only bored but also contemptuous, so he is imagining he's having sex with a librarian he's been flirting with, and whom he will later attempt to kill (if you haven't seen the show, believe it or not, that actually isn't a spoiler because he does this *every single time*, and if you haven't recognized that by the third season, I'm sorry for your loss).

What this means for me, practically speaking, is that the director wants a close-up of my face as my character Joe is deep in dissociative reverie mid-coitus. The camera, a very large apparatus weighing just about seven hundred pounds—lovely coincidence—does not allow space for itself and my scene partner (Victoria Pedretti, who brilliantly played Love in seasons 3 and 4 of *You*, and who is more beloved than I am by many fans of the show). If anyone or anything has to go, it won't be the camera; it will be my scene partner who sits this one out. This means that rather than simulating sex with her and looking at her while the camera watches us together, I'm going to have to simulate sex by myself, effectively humpin' on the air, on a fake bed in a fake room, surrounded by a film crew. Oh, and I'll be in the same nude thong I've been wearing all morning as we complete the scene, of course.

Because this is not my first rodeo, I've realized all of this before the director explains anything to me. I can see that it's what the shot requires, and it's a good shot. That's fine and clear. So, the director—a thoughtful and talented woman named Silver Tree—approaches me before she says anything to the camera department about what the shot will need. I appreciate her deference to me here. I'm in a robe (nude thong on underneath) and flip-flops. Like everyone else in a sound stage, Silver is fully dressed in sweater, jeans, and boots with an N95 mask on. Whereas one can see nearly all of me when I disrobe for the scene, all I can see of Silver is her eyes—but that's all I need. I can detect a sweetly nervous smile underneath her mask, and just a hint of (utterly professional) mischief. I know what she wants, and she knows I know, and she knows that I already agree it's what the scene needs. So, she shuffles up to me, almost doing a two-step, as she says, "Penn—"

I cut her off, gently. "You're putting the camera in my face."

She nods. "Yep."

"Victoria can't be there."

"Nope," she says, and clasps her hands behind her back diplomatically.

I chuckle, adjusting the waistband of my robe. "So, I'm going to be . . ."

She chuckles, too. "Mm-hmm . . ." It is her ellipsis which hangs in the air that surprises me, though. I pause. Silver's eyes shine, and I realize—

"You want me to look in camera, don't you?"

Silver's slow and silent nod is at once confident, demure, sheepish, and respectful. It will be one of my fondest memories of her when the series is long finished. We both laugh heartily now. Not only will I be humping the air with the camera in my face, but I'm going to be looking straight down the barrel of the lens, something I reflexively never do. You never let a mean girl know you're looking. Looking in camera ruins a take. Looking in camera is crossing a great metaphysical threshold because you've acknowledged the audience. The spell so delicately, exhaustively, extravagantly cast is broken with only a glance—unless, in rare circumstances, it works. This is one of those rare circumstances, made rarer by the fact that I will be simulating sex with the camera and, by proxy, the audience. For me, it would be truly naive to not consider now, even briefly, that—like so many other moments captured of me performing on this show—this one may very well become a meme.

I have a few minutes while they set up, and I don't think about it much. Not the point of the scene or the possibility of my body, a spectacle, living in a corner of the internet, infinitely humpin' on a GIF that sixteen-year-olds can use in a group chat. Now comes a young production assistant, totally overworked, underpaid, ambitious, stressed-out, masked up, her cargo pockets bulging with water bottles and script pages (should I ever need either one), a coiled plastic earpiece crammed into her ear canal connected to the walkie-talkie that is clipped to her utility belt and crackling incessantly with the urgent demands of any and every one her senior in any department—which is literally everyone on a film set—and so calmly, so kindly, this production assistant says to me, as she has hundreds or thousands of times this season:

"Camera is ready."

"Thank you, Jessica."

I have another thirty seconds to not really think about the scene, or any of the broader implications of what my work entails, as I walk from my Gore-Tex foldup camping chair in a dark corner of the soundstage to the bedroom set. The set is meant to look like a beautiful home, and it does. The entire crew has been working to make sure that it is beautiful, and to help the audience forget it's not real. Here, the camera and sound crew make final adjustments to their highly specialized machinery that will capture my performance. I nod at Victoria as she sits on a little wooden apple box to the side of the bed, wearing her own robe and flip-flops that match mine, an N95 mask on. Her eyes give me an encouraging smile (she'll have to do this, too, in the next camera setup).

Two women, both wearing full parkas and beanies, masks on, come to glance at my face and hair. I've not been wearing a mask while we film my side of the scene because it would leave telling marks on my face that the camera would see, and which would break the spell for the audience. The camera won't allow it.

"I look great, let's be honest." We laugh, and they scurry away as

I begin to untie my robe and step out of my flip-flops. A wardrobe assistant approaches in her fleece hoodie and hiking boots, and we nod at each other as she whisks away said robe and flip-flops. On a stage of at least one hundred people dressed like they are going camping on a cold October day, all in medical-grade masks during a global pandemic, some of whose faces I will *never* see, I am now as nude as I was born but for a flimsy thong, and this is my work.

I've made it, I tell myself. Little Penn would be awed and humbled.

I kneel onto the thin, false mattress where the camera rig—a large and unwieldy apparatus—hovers on a jib arm that extends from a Transformer-esque machine, one that is modified from the original Moviola Crab Dolly that used to load bombs into planes during World War II.* The whole setup looks like a giant creature with an extremely dense and compact body, a long, protruding neck, and an almost-cute face—a little bit like Wall-E, and a little bit like the servant-pet-robot from *Red Planet* that turns on Val Kilmer and tries to murder him. This is my pretend lover for the next ten to fifteen minutes.

The crew has quieted respectfully, as they always do, and there is an impossible silence inside a twenty-thousand-square-foot space crowded with people and electronic equipment. On the bed, I shuffle on my knees toward the camera, my lover forged from metal and glass hovering just above a down pillow with a four-hundred-fifty-thread-count pillowcase. As I approach, I get onto all fours, scooching myself closer so that the camera is beneath me and looking right up at me. I've not yet turned my face to peer into its eye. There are the

---

* Whether those dollies are loaded with bombs in the early twentieth century, or a camera rig and its camera operator in our new millennium, it *keeps* adding up to just about seven hundred pounds.

strangest of butterflies flitting in my stomach. I realize as I try to look into the lens that, for a moment, I can't. I simply cannot. It's too bald, too bold, too bawdy; and I feel naked because I am almost naked. I really can't take this seriously. I start to giggle, and then I laugh, quaking on all fours. Every part of me that can jiggle is now jiggling. Our camera operator starts to laugh, and so does the sound guy holding a boom mic just above my head. We all laugh, and it's a relaxing, unifying moment. But we must quiet, and eventually we do.

I finally look into the lens. *You* (my show, not my reader) uses these beautiful, old anamorphic lenses from classic film cameras—somewhat rare these days. The thick, meticulously distorted glass in the barrel captures and reflects light in subtle and enchanting lines like an artistic rendering of a black hole in space. The depth of blackness inside the lens is unnatural—in fact, it is pitch-black surrounding the very center, where a perfectly round dot glows with the faintest red light, like a thin membrane, a veil between me and the other side (and the audience). The lens is such a sensitive and powerful mechanism that it usually needs to be encased by a dulled metal frame with little flippered visors on it. This is called a matte box. It fits over the lens like a picture frame so the visors can flip out to shield the lens from any light that would hit it directly and create ghostly shapes in camera.

Beholding the matte box, I notice that as it casts the lens in shadow, all the dimension I could see before in the lens is now gone. I realize this little black box has momentarily hidden from me the true nature and intensity of the seven-hundred-pound apparatus of blown and curved glass, brushed metal, and intricate circuitry, here to record everything I do. It appears the eye is closed; the mirror is shrouded. This is not typically its purpose, but today the little black box has made me just a bit more comfortable as a I continue my life's work.

The time has come for me to hump.

"*Action.*" Silver's delivery is, possibly, more delicate than mine will be.

I'm not home, but I can imagine that I am. There is no one in front of me, but I can imagine someone is. A moment ago there was only resistance in my body to do what was needed, but upon the utterance of one word—*action*—I am supremely present in the face of sheer absurdity. I look in camera. And I hump my ass off.

In camera is an archaic Latin phrase used in law, translated literally as "in a chamber," but which means, very simply, "in private" because the litigators or whomever would retreat to a private chamber to discuss matters that would not be disclosed to the press or the public. That's the most important part of the premise: not to be seen. They already knew what physicists would discover centuries later—the imposing power of observation. I have learned this, too. If I was an intent observer as a boy, I have become intently observed as a man. It's a role reversal I can't undo, and the only way forward is to distinguish self-awareness from self-consciousness, self-mastery from self-idolatry, self-abnegation from self-flagellation.

And of all the reversals of intent, or developments of culture, that might mystify the progenitors of our social systems centuries ago—men in wigs and leggings who could never have anticipated the religious fervor that celebrity inculcates in its millions of adherents—the evolution of this two-word, tetrasyllabic phrase might dazzle them most: *in camera.*

(And, scene.)

A FAMILY RECIPE

NAVA

Ingredients for breaking your mother's heart:

2 chicken breasts
1 onion
2 cloves garlic
3 cups basmati rice
3 egg yolks
1 cup plain yogurt
¼ cup butter

4 tbsp saffron
¼ cup zereshk (barberries)
1 tbsp sugar
1 tsp turmeric
1 pinch salt
1 splash frozen orange juice concentrate

. . .

It's a Wednesday night and I'm attempting to make *tahcheen* for the first time without my mom's help. Mom passed away a decade ago, and the only time we ever made it together was when I was still in my early twenties. It's been at least fifteen years since I've made this dish. I'm peering into the pan, trying to remember how much orange juice she added to her barberries. I can't google this particular step because it was her secret ingredient.

It's eight p.m. in Los Angeles, which means it's too late in Sweden, where Zhena lives, for me to ask her, and Dad doesn't remember this little trick.

"Do you mean when she used orange zest in her *fesenjān*?"

No, I don't. In fact, I have no recollection of how she made *fesenjān* at all. My heart sinks a little, but I press on. I remember that she had a trick for the *tahcheen* that involved setting aside the barberries and cooking them in frozen, concentrated OJ, but I just can't remember how much she used and at what point she added the barberries back into the rest of the dish.

I feel the tears forming.

Why, oh why, was I such a stubborn child?

My mother made a significant effort to try to get me to cook with her when I was growing up. Cooking was her passion. She was so good at it, and she did it with extraordinary love. She wanted very badly for us to bond over it, and I simply resisted. I resisted as a child. I resisted as a teenager. As an adult, when most of the rebellion had left my body and four years of full-time service in Haifa had more or less exorcised the taunt-your-sweet-mother demons out of me, the slight concession I made to her obvious desire was agreeing to bake with her on special occasions.

If I had to guess—and I have to, because she's dead (yes, I will play that card as often as I can), I think one of her happiest memories with me was when we baked my dad's sixty-fifth-birthday cake together. I had suggested we bake an ambitious, three-tiered, dark-chocolate raspberry cake. She was so patient and kind as she explained even the most basic steps to me. She had a sweet smile on her face the entire time and would spontaneously pull me toward her and hug me throughout the process. At one point, when I got particularly frustrated over my own inefficacy, she kissed my forehead and said, *"Kam kam, ruz beh ruz."* ("Little by little, day by day.")

This was a particularly special event because, until I was twenty-three years old, I didn't even know how to hard-boil an egg. (I surreptitiously googled that in an apartment in Beijing, too humiliated to ask one of my roommates at the time.)

Growing up in Farahnaz Kavelin's home without knowing how to hard-boil an egg required effort. Firstly, we were not spoiled. My mom was a huge fan of children having chores. ("Accustom your children to hardship" may have been her favorite quote.) Secondly, she was *always* cooking, and she welcomed our involvement. Finally, every other member of my family was a wonderful cook. It was as though I'd opted to put on a blindfold every time I stepped into the kitchen from the ages of five—probably how old Zhena[*] was when *she* learned how to hard-boil an egg—to eighteen.

So back to present-day Nava, attempting to make *tahcheen* for the first time on her own. The last time I made it fifteen years ago, I didn't know it would be my *last time* making it with Mom, so I can't say that I recall much about the experience. I'm certain she would have been patient and smiling that special smile she saved for the rare nights I agreed to spend time cooking with her.

I very badly wish they hadn't been so rare.

I guess I'll just eyeball it . . .

---

[*] Zhena and her two sons, Naim and Zane, make pancakes and eggs together on weekends, and the boys have been helping her since they were four years old. I've never told her, or anyone, that to this day, I've still never made a pancake. And I *do* eat gluten.

I pull out a tablespoon and start sprinkling juice onto the barberries.

As the barberries start to sizzle, I am overcome by a different memory of *tahcheen*. This one is painful.

• • •

My mom was a stay-at-home parent. She was incredibly loving and she was fluent in all the so-called love languages, but if I had to pick one as her strongest, it would be acts of service. Her favorite act of service was to cook.

Our kitchen was *small*, and for most of our early childhood there was no AC in our apartment. It would get so hot in there! Mama often emerged from the kitchen with sweaty hair stuck to her head.

Mom's main way of spoiling us was with food. Each member of the family had an individual favorite dish. Our collective favorite was *tahcheen*. *Tahcheen* requires a heavy dose of saffron. In addition to being expensive, Persian saffron wasn't sold in Puerto Rico when I was growing up, and Amazon was not a thing yet. My mom's relatives and best friends would send her care packages that included that precious spice. While Mom was incredibly generous, she wanted the saffron to last, so the saffron-centric meals came much less frequently than other Persian dishes. It was always special when she made *tahcheen*.

My mom knew I had a giant, years-long crush on Diego. I mean, everyone knew. But so did my mom. We rarely spoke of it, but one night during my junior year of high school when she learned he was coming over with a couple of other boys, Santiago and Mateo, to work on a group project, she decided to surprise us with *tahcheen*. She wanted to help me make a good impression.

"It's dinnertime," she called out a couple of hours after Diego, Santiago, and I had been working. When we emerged from my room and went into the kitchen where the *tahcheen* was waiting, she looked at me expectantly. I started to smile, but the boys were immediately suspicious.

Tahcheen looks like an upside-down pineapple cake if the top were made of crispy rice. The inside layers consist of chicken breasts, barberries, and basmati rice that is moist with saffron, yogurt, and egg yolk.

They'd never seen a dish like it.

"What is this?" Diego asked timidly.

"It's really delicious! *Te va encantar!*" I responded.

Once the *tahcheen* was served, I dug into my portion with relish, but I noticed the boys eating a little more slowly. They were sneaking glances at each other.

I looked down at my plate and noticed the *zereshk* (barberries). I figured sour little berries could be off-putting if you're not expecting them.

"You can pick around the berries," I offered.

They both smiled and said nothing.

Finally, we went back into my bedroom to hang out.

Mateo, the last member of our group project, always late, arrived and came straight to my room.

"Any leftovers?" he asked.

"Yup! A bunch! Please have some!" I left to grab a drink from the kitchen.

As soon as I left the room, I heard Diego and Santiago start laughing. I paused outside the closed door. "Don't eat the rice!" Diego cried out. Santiago referred to it as "timcheen." "I think they put . . . gum in it?" Diego added. He and Santiago were laughing hysterically at this point—and trading notes on how awful the rice was. "Gum and sour berries!" he added.

I fought back tears but went into the kitchen to get a drink and try to collect myself before heading back to the room. I smiled at Mateo as we passed each other in the hallway. Despite his laughter, he tried the *tahcheen* anyway. Maybe to see how bad it was? He made himself a small bowl, and by all accounts, actually enjoyed it.

But *Diego* hated it. Diego thought it was weird. Diego thought my mom put chewing gum in his rice. (The yogurt and egg yolk made the rice sticky. That was actually my favorite part, and I usually added *more* yogurt to it.)

When the boys left, I marched straight to my mom, who was washing dishes in the kitchen, and unleashed on her.

"WHY DID YOU HAVE TO MAKE *TAHCHEEN*! YOU HUMILIATED ME IN FRONT OF MY FRIENDS!"

My mother was taken completely aback.

"*Tahcheen* is your favorite dish!"

"BUT I'M PERSIAN! I'M USED TO *WEIRD FOOD*! MY FRIENDS AREN'T! WHY COULDN'T YOU JUST HAVE MADE NORMAL CHICKEN!" I stormed off, still screaming. I locked myself in my room and finished my homework.

A couple of hours later, at bedtime, I left my room to go to the hallway bathroom, right next to the primary bedroom, to brush my teeth. My parents' door was closed. I heard crying. I stepped gently to the door and pressed my ear against it.

"Tommy, I spent hours on that dish! I thought she would be happy! Nothing I do is ever right with Nava."

My instant reaction was to open the door and hug her, comfort her. I was wrong. I was projecting all my insecurities on her. It was all me. But I kept my feet planted on the ground. My dad tried to soothe her.

"It's just a teenage thing, Farahnaz. She doesn't mean it . . ." My mom appeared to be inconsolable. I stood there for a full minute trying to summon the courage to open the door and apologize.

Finally, I sneaked into the bathroom. Brushed my teeth. Left. Paused outside my parents' door once more. Walked back to my room and slipped under the covers. Never apologized. Never even acknowledged that it happened.

At seventeen, all I could think about was how to fit in, how to shrink myself down to avoid being the girl with the "weird" Persian mom who made "weird" Persian food. I wanted to blend seamlessly into my friends' lives, to avoid any reminder that I was different. I loved my culture, but in that moment I wanted to pretend I wasn't Persian. That I was just like everyone else. The boys' laughter stung because, deep down, I feared they were right. That maybe our food was strange. Maybe *I* was strange.

Food, especially when it's tied to culture, is never just about sustenance. It's a language of its own, one that speaks volumes about where we come from, what we value, and how we love. In my home, *tahcheen* was more than a dish; it was my mother's way of keeping her Persian heritage alive in a place where we collectively didn't always fit in. It wasn't just saffron, yogurt, and rice; it was the hours of patience, the painstaking care, and the invisible string that tied our family to a homeland far away.

• • •

My alarm goes off. It's time to pull the *tahcheen* out of the oven. The trickiest part of the whole endeavor is next: flipping it over and onto a tray. This is the moment you learn if you used enough butter, if your dish was in the oven long enough, if the rice has crisped properly.

I flip the dish and . . . nothing. It does not come sliding out. I fight back tears as I realize I've messed something up.

"I'm so proud of you for trying, Nava joon." Mama's voice comes to mind. I can so clearly picture her drawing me into her for a hug, a sweet smile forming on her face, as she patiently explains I probably needed more butter. She would have kissed my forehead and said—

"Kam kam ruz beh ruz." (Little by little, day by day.)

. . .

2 chicken breasts
1 onion
2 cloves garlic
3 cups basmati rice
3 egg yolks
1 cup plain yogurt
1/4 cup butter

4 tbsp saffron
1/4 cup zereshk (barberries)
1 tbsp sugar
1 tsp turmeric
1 pinch salt
1 splash frozen orange juice concentrate

Ingredients for showing your daughter how much you love her.

COOL GIRL

SOPHIE

My phone pinged from across the room. It was an Instagram message from Lucia. Outside of the salon birthday fiasco, I had fond memories of Lucia, but that didn't change the fact that we hadn't spoken in almost two decades. It turned out she'd moved to Los Angeles not too long ago, so we decided to meet for coffee.

I arrived at the café early, rolling my stroller around the steps and up the ramp. I was thirty years old, married, and a new mother. I was about as adult as it gets. But a familiar feeling started to wash over me, and it didn't matter how settled I felt in my adulthood: the insecurity of middle school still radiated from deep in my core, out to my fingertips. I fiddled with my shirt, and then my phone and then my hair, until Lucia's familiar voice called out to me. She looked chic in a black tank and low-slung jeans. Suddenly I was self-conscious about my fully thrifted outfit.

We swapped life updates. She had started a new job in marketing; I had just gotten the hang of breastfeeding. She was hunting down the perfect finishings for her new solo apartment, and I was celebrating four consecutive hours of sleep.

Even though Lucia was living in LA now, she had maintained close relationships with many of our old classmates, visiting them for holidays, going on trips, and celebrating big life events. She gave me the scoop on all our friends from middle school. Grace was set to marry in the summer. Michelle had moved home and was on the brink of divorce. My middle school "boyfriend," with whom I had exchanged no more than ten words while we were together, had finally come out to his family! I lapped up every word.

She asked about our podcast, *Podcrushed*, and we laughed about how ridiculous it seemed that I was cohosting it with *the* Penn Badgley. We had watched *Gossip Girl* together, episode by episode, as they'd come out. Two of our friends, Grace and Mari, had even referred to themselves as B and S, after Blair and Serena in the show.

Sitting at the coffee shop in LA, Lucia told me she'd never liked Penn's character in the show. Dan Humphrey, who hailed from Brooklyn to join the old-money, Upper East Side students at a prep school in Manhattan on scholarship, seemed insecure to Lucia, and that was annoying to her. I laughed along at the seemingly casual comment, but inside something clicked for me. I had never perceived Dan as insecure because I, effectively, *was* Dan. I saw him as a kid who was out of his element and giving up parts of himself to keep up in a world that wasn't his and never would be. I saw him as a victim in the whole scenario, and I felt bad for him; I was never annoyed by him. But Lucia was right—Dan was insecure, and so was I.

It brought me right back to middle school in Manila.

There's a common Tagalog term that I learned very quickly after moving to the Philippines: *barkada*. Your *barkada* is your tight-knit group of friends who stick with you for life. I think the fact that there's a specific word for a lifelong friend group that goes through every stage together says something about Filipino culture. I moved to Manila as an expat and was never going to stay for more than a handful of years before my father's next posting with the UN, so by definition I was never going to be fully inducted into a *barkada*, no matter how hard I tried.

Thirteen-year-old Sophie was exuberant, sometimes nauseatingly chatty, and had a mouth full of retainers. Our family had lived in Manila for almost four years by the time I was thirteen, which was by far the longest I had ever lived in one place. That should have been my clue that our next move was imminent. But when my parents told us we were heading to China, it was the shock of a lifetime.

Up until this point, I had loved moving from country to country. It had given me a chance to meet a whole new crop of kids, which meant endless opportunity and an exciting adventure ahead. But this time it felt different. For starters, it was the middle of eighth grade and things were going well for me in Manila. Remember Lucia's exclusive salon birthday party? That was just the start for me. By the time I was in eighth grade, I had been taken fully under the wing of *the* Grace Gutierrez. Grace was the ringleader of the popular crew, and under her were Lucia, Mari, and a smattering of other girls.

Grace was undeniably the coolest and prettiest girl in school. Even though I feared her more than I loved her, her co-sign gave me a kind of social status I welcomed. Once she decided she liked me, I was at all the birthday parties, all the sleepovers, and I even scored an invite for a weekend away at one of her family's many weekend homes. I was exposed to a life totally different from my own, and while I wasn't sure if I liked it—I could already tell I was out of my depth and didn't quite fit in—I knew that it was rare for someone like me to be brought into the fold. So I zipped it, and accepted it.

While my family was firmly in the middle class, not wanting for much, all things are relative, and these kids had private jets and pool houses. I had been ushered into a new world of holiday beach homes, chauffeurs, and social capital, oh my! It was exhilarating and, for the first time, moving to a new country was the last thing I wanted. Besides—my sunk costs were piling up. I had already given up several friends that I had grown close to over the previous years in order to be initiated into Grace Gutierrez's crew. It seemed cruel that in one instant I would lose all the ground I'd gained. What I didn't know was that, while I was pledging my loyalty to this new friend group, one of its members was already plotting my downfall.

Grace Gutierrez's cool-girls-only social circle was complex, stratified, and governed by a set of unwritten rules. Grace herself was the queen, pulling strings between the girls and still somehow convincing us she was unaware of the power dynamics at play. The responsibility of enforcement was left to her fixer and consigliere, Mari Flores—perhaps the only person I feared more than Grace.

Mari was clever and calculating. She seemed to take a sadistic sort of pleasure in bringing others down. Having said that, I'd be lying if I claimed I never participated in her antics. When she whispered mean things about our classmates at school, I whispered back. Gossip is intoxicating—a surefire way to feel a superficial connection with someone you can't quite figure out. But the brief connection I'd feel with Mari over gossip never lasted long, and it always seemed to leave me feeling icky. Maybe it left her feeling the same way.

Mari took the old adage "Keep your friends close and your enemies closer" to heart. We lived in the same apartment building, and she invited me over often, getting to know me well. In the time we spent together, Mari was careful to remind me in subtle ways of the power she had. She would lord her position over me in intangible ways that I didn't quite pick up on until later in life. For instance, Mari knew that I was obsessed with looking at photos; it was convenient that she always had the newest digital camera and an iMac with *thousands* of pictures of us and our classmates, cataloged neatly in folders. When I'd come over, I'd beg her to let me look through the photos. She seldom allowed it. But when she did, she made sure to keep control over the mouse, and no matter how into it I was, she would unexpectedly quit iPhoto whenever she deemed we'd had enough. Small actions like this one solidified our ranks in relation to each other.

Despite some of my unnerving experiences with Mari, I never expected to become one of her targets.

When my parents officially told me we'd be picking up and leaving our lives in Manila for Beijing, I did what any thirteen-year-old girl would do—I cried to my friends about it, and they cried with me. Including Mari, whose plan was already in motion.

We landed in Beijing late at night in early January. I was plucked from balmy, tropical Manila and dropped into a gray and hazy city that was well below 0 degrees Celsius. We rode in a white van from the airport to the temporary one-bedroom apartment our family of five would live in for the next month while we searched for permanent housing. We made a stop at the manager's office, and while my parents went inside to get the keys, my siblings and I sat in the van in silence. This was our seventh move. You'd think it would get easier with time, but for some reason this felt like the most jarring transition yet. I stared at the security guards in front of the van. They wore long army-green coats and fur hats. Everything was muted except for the bright-red ends of their cigarettes. The smoke looked exaggerated, spilling out of their mouths into the cold winter air.

I thought I was an expert new kid at this point in my life. I knew what fun facts made for a good icebreaker (*my first kiss was with a whale*) and how to spot a potential new friend (*someone loud and unusually into their stationery*). But this move felt distinctly different from the previous six.

Almost immediately upon starting school, a girl named Cove started a rumor that I had gotten a boob job, which was rich considering a) I was thirteen and b) I had a deep-rooted hatred for the stretch marks that ran down my chest, which meant that every single day I wore high-necked tops and hoodies. All I had ever wanted to do was shrink my body, every part of it . . . so a boob job? It was insulting.

After the rumor got back to me, I begged my mom for a breast reduction.

"You'll come to appreciate them," she told me without lifting her gaze from her book. (*Spoiler: I never did.* They have, in fact, remained a nuisance.)

That January, I found myself in a whole new pool of kids and, for the first time I didn't feel like swimming. The rumors about my body spread and morphed into rumors about who I liked and my supposed intentions to steal Cove's boyfriend. I didn't know how to defend myself when no one had known me for more than a few weeks, but I continued to deny and just hope that people took it at face value.

I started slipping into a depression. If it weren't for the whispers between my parents, I wouldn't have even known that's what it was. I didn't feel sad; I just didn't feel anything at all. This move was the straw that broke the camel's back, and suddenly I was over our nomadic lifestyle. I didn't want to make any effort to fit in, settle down, or make myself known.

"Honey, you have to get her to shower," my dad pleaded with my mom one day.

To her credit, she did try. "How about we wash your hair today, my love?" she suggested ever so gently.

I scraped my tangled hair into a bun for the eighth day in a row. "Not today," I muttered.

All that kept me going was the promise of a visit back to Manila at the end of the school year. With four months to go, I was counting down the days. But plans changed, and even though my parents tried to let me down easy, I took it hard.

I did the only thing I could to communicate my anger: I declared a hunger strike. Very youngest child of me, I know. The great hunger strike of 2008 has gone down as the quickest and quietest protest in Rutstein family history. When I skipped dinner that night, my father made one of his special sandwiches. He has a talent for sandwich building; it is a very precise science for him. We have often suggested that his third act in life should be opening his own sandwich shop. How could I resist? He quietly placed the food outside my bedroom door. When he returned an hour later, all that was left were a few crumbs on an empty plate.

Just like my hunger strike, my struggle to settle into life in Beijing was extreme, but short-lived. A couple of months into our move, I began to find my people, including one Maggie Saunders. I got to know Maggie slowly, over several months in group hangs. And it wasn't until we had an established friendship that I found out my reputation in Beijing had preceded me.

It turned out that the rumor Cove had started about my preteen boob job would soon be old news. There was a separate, unrelated rumor that was waiting to be spread by someone I thought was an old friend.

In the days before my move, Mari from Manila had found the one person she knew distantly in Beijing, Maggie Saunders, and taken it upon herself to reach out. Mari had realized that I'd be going to the same school as Maggie, and she'd emailed her with a formal request to make sure I wouldn't make any new friends there. To this day I am unsure why Mari tried to poison the water from afar before I even had a chance to swim. I, of course, was totally unaware of this. While I was busy processing the transition I was about to make, Mari was doing what she could to make sure I'd never fit in. Lucky for me, Maggie was a year older and many years wiser, and she saw Mari's request for what it was—an unfair and bitter plea. She read the email, clicked delete, and never did a thing about it.

I felt betrayed by Mari, of course. But another feeling quickly took its place—relief. In the years I had spent with Grace Gutierrez's crew, I'd always been on edge. It had felt like I was *working* to be someone who could be worthy of their acceptance. And in the search for their approval, I had given up real friendships where I felt free to be my full self.

My memories with those friends from early middle school are distinctly different from those with Grace's crew. I had friends who were more my speed in the earlier years. We made up dances too complicated for our uncoordinated limbs to match. And when we forced our parents to watch us perform them, we hardly noticed their disinterest. We blew up kiddy pools in backyards and jumped in with all our clothes on, pretending we were grown-ups in a hot tub. When we got tired of splashing, we sprawled out on the grass to dry off. Heads together and eyes closed under the blazing sun, we made up nonsensical jokes that we couldn't explain. We stuck exercise balls under giant sleep shirts and ran at each other to see how far we'd bounce back. For science.

I wince thinking about how easily I dropped my friends when the opportunity for popularity was dangled in front of me. I started accepting invitations from Grace, Lucia, and co. that conflicted with the plans of my original friends until eventually I was out of one group and in the other.

When I think back to middle school, those memories of unbridled joy and silliness are the ones I cherish most. In contrast, the insecurity that I felt while trying to fit in with Grace's group overrode whatever silliness existed. The moment Maggie told me about Mari's email, the veil was lifted and I saw how fleeting, stressful, and ultimately *boring* the "cool girl" identity was.

Looking back, letting go of my real friendships in search of cooler ones is my biggest regret from adolescence. I think about those original friends from Manila often and wonder how they're doing. Sometimes I think of Mari, too. I wonder what she must have felt like inside. What could push someone to do something so cold? When I was thirteen, I saw her as powerful, confident, and cool. In my mind she had everything I was lacking. But with more than a few years of distance, I realize she must have been just as insecure as I had been.

There isn't really any use in trying to figure out why Mari did what she did. I'm not sure that it can be tied to anything rational, and the chances are that if I were to reach out to her now and ask her about it, she might not even remember. But *I do*.

Recalling the dynamics of my friendship with Grace, Mari, and Lucia gives me some understanding of who I am today. Unpacking the experiences that have echoed through the years brings up important questions for me. Why do I remember this specific detail? How is this dynamic playing out for me as an adult? What blind spot is this pushing up against?

It's taken many years for me to shake off the insecurity underneath my need for acceptance, and some days I realize I'm still in the process of doing this. I catch myself trying to morph into someone that I *think* will garner attention from a person I feel the need to impress.

Over coffee with Lucia, I saw traces of my middle school self.

In that one comment about Dan Humphrey, I remembered that Lucia and I had had two entirely different experiences of middle school. She was the fish who didn't recognize the water. When you're *in*, you don't even know there is an *out*. Her place was locked in by virtue of her class and her generations-old family history in the Philippines. *Barkada* status. And by the same token, if I hadn't been so preoccupied with my positioning, I might have realized no one saw me as an outsider quite as much as I did.

I told Lucia that I was in the midst of writing about what Mari did back in eighth grade. She had a vague memory of the events, and although she couldn't remember exactly what went down, she wasn't surprised. "I don't mix with her anymore," she said. That was news to me. Lucia continued, "Mari has mean girl energy." *That* part I could have told you.

Despite my initial nerves and my incessant fiddling, seeing Lucia was refreshing. By the end of our coffee, the insecurity had mostly melted away. Before Lucia and I parted ways, we said we should get together again, but it's been nearly a year and neither of us has reached out to meet up. I can't speak for her, but if I had to guess why, I'd say we both recognized how different our lives are now, and we've accepted that middle school memories alone might not be enough to go off of.

I've made many mistakes in my friendships over the years. I have taken friends for granted, let the ball slip, and failed to communicate how much they mean to me. I have a handful of friendships that I treasure, and I think those people know how much I cherish them. But on the whole, I am still learning how to be a good friend, which is a hard thing to admit. I have written and deleted that sentence three times because I'm nervous about how it makes me look. What does it say about me that I have lost many friends along the way?

What is clear to me at thirty is that friendships aren't static—they shift, fade, and sometimes surprise you by reappearing when you don't expect it. It's the ebb and flow, the entrances and exits, that shape us just as much as the ones who stay, reminding me that every connection, brief or lasting, leaves its mark.

My friendships have carried me through boredom, heartbreak,

tragedy, loneliness, and the monotony and magic of motherhood. The truth is that I wouldn't be standing without my friends past and present, so I'm hanging on tightly to the ones I've kept, and taking this as a reminder to build new connections where I can.

Through my friends I see myself, and they have taught me that the version of me worth holding on to is the one who values what's real over what glitters.

FORTY DAYS AND FORTY NIGHTS

PENN

My mother and I sat in the principal's office of John Burroughs High School in Burbank, California, just a few weeks shy of the school year's start. The principal, a thoughtful and modest woman in her forties, looked at me from across her desk with a bit of perplexity and less curiosity than I'd hoped. She then looked at her colleague, another modest woman sitting toward the corner of their fluorescent-lit office, who could only offer an optimistic shrug.

"Well, what grade would you like to be in?"

Typically very shy, this was the sort of space in which I had no nerves. I chuckled like I'd been on a press circuit for weeks and answered affably, "I've been thinking about this. Ninth grade seems too young"—I was, in fact, only thirteen years old, the age of many eighth graders—"But I want to go to high school for as long as I can. So, I was thinking that I could be a sophomore?"

I shouldn't have asked it like a question, but what could they say? I already had the equivalent of a high school diploma, according to the State of California. Earlier that year, I'd passed the California

High School Proficiency Exam because my mother and I had seen what homeschooling in Hollywood was like while I was auditioning constantly and working sporadically during our first year there. I took the CHSPE to prove and protect myself, so that when I worked on a movie or television show, I wouldn't have to spend three hours a day on set with a tutor after I wrapped. I could also work a full twelve-hour shift or more, like any adult on a film set. This was a major asset for a young actor in a lineup of kids who could only work eight hours at most and would require a tutor. That, and I also preferred it, because it gave me the freedom to go to community college early if everything started falling apart.

Still relatively bright-eyed and bushy-tailed, however, I wanted it all. I wanted to act, yes, but I wanted to go to high school, too. I wanted normalcy. My mother was working full-time at a Home Depot on Sunset Boulevard in Hollywood, and until I took the CHSPE, I was in a government-funded homeschooling program that gave each student a free, giant, blocky desktop computer with a convex, bubble-screen, monochrome monitor that displayed a neon-green MS-DOS typeface. Any work I tried do on that machine was staggeringly tedious. I felt like I was coding against my will, at a time when coding was not cool.

When I was assigned to read the entire Magna Carta on it, I tapped out. I would have gleaned more from the original in Latin on calfskin vellum, or from a lobotomy. I had always been an academic kid and couldn't have conceived of not doing my schoolwork before this, let alone cutting class, but this homeschool program made me feel like Judd Nelson in *The Breakfast Club*. It was maddening, and I found there was no way to motivate myself through it, despite having monthly check-ins with a woman named April who must have been a social worker. Shout-out to you, April, doing God's work on Job's pay. I'm sorry that I did not read the Magna Carta like I was supposed to.

My mother and I had spent that first year in Los Angeles—what would have been my eighth-grade year—living in a trailer park in North Hollywood, so far north that it is technically called Sun Valley. These were the industrial bowels of the huge San Bernardino Valley in Los Angeles County, the same valley where Alicia Silverstone was mugged and stranded in *Clueless*, the same valley where I would live for the duration of my teenage years and which borders Hollywood both as a state of mind and as a place. My homeschooling days in Sun Valley were spent cruising the lanes of the trailer park on Rollerblades, skateboard, or bike with a few boys my age, and we had some prematurely explicit times for twelve- and thirteen-year-olds. I had my first encounters with alcohol, marijuana, and the female anatomy within my first week of living there. I was far too young for all three and absolutely thrilled about it. Furthermore, it was the first time I felt part of a crew of my peers. Performing in community theater back in Washington had been a revelation for the fellowship it offered, especially for its mixed ages and the full-blown adults with whom I had formed professional relationships. But here I was part of a clan of young people who roamed the park—about fifteen of us in total—all ranging from twelve to eighteen years old. That kind of comradery was genuinely new for me. I wasn't at all dissuaded or dispirited by the dangers that lurked on the periphery of our youthful group. That lot, outwardly destitute, was an oasis in the industrial disintegration that surrounded it, and I felt safe because I was part of a community.

This was the same year that Eminem's debut record, *The Slim*

Shady LP, was selling millions of units. He was a fellow white boy who came from a trailer park, and I hoped this was not where our similarities ended. He was sexy, quick-witted, and a genius. Everyone loved him, and yet he had suffered a lot in his adolescence. I purchased his CD at the record store across the street from the Home Depot where my mom worked, bluffing for the guy at checkout when he asked me if my parents knew I was buying it. I nodded solemnly and said, "Yes." I may be a decent actor, but I've never been a good liar. He scrutinized me, and I felt a chill. There was not one ounce of charm in our exchange.

"Well, you can't return this if they find out." He shrugged, and I shrugged back at him. I walked out staring in awe at the shrink-wrapped jewel case that would become my most prized possession and that my mother would find a few weeks later on a sad night that was the beginning of the end of our time living in the trailer park.

On this night, as I came home through the sliding glass door that was our only entrance to the double-wide we lived in—cushy compared to my friends' places—I found my mother sitting in one of the wicker chairs that typically surrounded the dining table. Now it was positioned in front of the door, one half of an interrogation that hadn't started yet. She sat there with an unusual stoicism, holding *The Slim Shady LP* jewel case. I had walked into an ambush.

She demanded that I get my Discman, so I did, and I watched with rising dread as she slid my headphones over her graying mane and onto her ears to listen to *The Slim Shady LP* for the first (and probably only) time. She cradled her head with one hand as the other clenched my Discman, and I was able to listen along with her to the barely audible treble of each high hat and snare. I rapped silently in my head to keep track with her so I could brace myself for the lyrics I thought would be the worst from her perspective. This is a hallmark of adolescence: believing you understand where your parents are coming from, and also believing that they couldn't possibly imagine where *you* are coming from.

Neither my mother nor I can remember what her punishment for buying Eminem's CD was, and I concede with utter humility now—as a father myself, and a sensible adult regardless—that her horror at his lyrics was justified. She clearly felt there were myriad negative influences converging on her only son at a critical time in his life, and soon after that night she started looking for apartments in a different neighborhood (where kids probably listened to *more* Eminem). Also, critically, I had started working and making enough money to contribute in small part to monthly expenses. This helped us find a nicer place to live.

We moved from the trailer park into an apartment complex in a suburb called Burbank, which is much closer to Hollywood itself and whose economy is upheld by the proliferation of studio lots like Universal, Disney, and Warner Brothers. It was certainly a nicer area, but it wasn't where I wanted to spend my days cruising. If I wasn't going to have another lawless gap year, I wanted classes with teachers, chemistry tests, band practice, my first girlfriend, school dances, and autumnal walks home with a heavy backpack. For this, John Burroughs High School was the only choice I had.

Burroughs wasn't an incredible school, but it was a solid one. It had one claim to fame, that Ron Howard went there—Ron Howard, of *Happy Days* and Hollywood legacy, one of the most acclaimed and celebrated directors of the last century. This gave me the vaguest of impressions that I, too, might rise from obscurity and make something of myself in this ol' star-spangled town. So, I enrolled at John Burroughs High School and was very excited to be—after having already played one on television—a true high schooler.

I was also intensely self-conscious about this shift. The truth is that I had not been going to school consistently since moving from my childhood home in Virginia to Washington State at eight years old. Even in Washington we had moved around a lot and, at first, lived in isolated rural areas where finding a decent school was a challenge. I spent most of my fourth-grade year out of school, and after completing my fifth- and sixth-grade years like a normal kid at a normal school, I couldn't complete my seventh-grade year before moving to Los Angeles. During those same years, I had gained a lot of weight and become quite chubby, and at one point—the year before entering high school—I was just plain fat. I was a fat little thirteen-year-old, which is worth noting because it was unnatural for my body type, even with puberty. It had been my depressive response to the slow dissolution of my parents' marriage and our family unit and a symptom of the magnified isolation I was experiencing with all the moving (it's hard to have friends when you're moving all the time). I was painfully sensitive about this extra weight I carried, and when I first saw myself on camera after booking my first role, I remember being shocked. I took being fat so personally. The first time I was called on an audition specifically to play the fat kid, I cried and refused to go.

Part of me, then, was terrified of what people would think of me in high school. I imagined classes being full of those lanky kids with default abs, flat and wide pecs, shaggy hair, and beautiful eyes. I was five foot five with at least an A cup, would be thirteen in tenth grade, and had zero friends where I was going.

For a short week that summer, I had been boyfriend-girlfriend with a girl from Texas who lived in my apartment complex, and she connected me to two other kids who went to Burroughs. This girl and I, we never kissed. We had failed to make out when all our friends wanted us to (while we were in Rollerblades and everyone else was on the other side of the door), so our relationship had felt like a disappointment for us, and for everybody. She was doing me a real solid introducing me to her two friends, kind of like an ex who co-parents better than she partners. And her two friends, my only portal to a social life at John Burroughs High School, were a power couple. Their names were Steven and Tessa, and they were both beautiful and bronzed and hot and I just wanted to have what they had. But even though I had somewhat of a friendship lifeline, I would have no classes with Steven, Tessa, or any of their friends. They were—appropriately—freshmen, and I'd be on my own as a very young sophomore.

I have no recollection of the classes themselves on my first day of high school, but I remember the hallways in between. They were a wide and coursing river of student bodies; over one thousand kids were hustling to their classes. It was overwhelming for everybody, and I looked around to try to read the faces of the river, wondering if I could do this for three more years, when I saw Steven. He was a rock in this body of water.

Steven played hockey. He was very strong and mature, both in body and mind, but he was not tall. I think he was about my height. And he demonstrated at fourteen years infinitely more wisdom and character than any freshman or sophomore I had met by our second period on the first day of school. As I made my way over to him, Steven was hip-checked by a friend of his—I think this guy even called out, "Hip-check!"—and Steven stumbled into the pathway of a very tall, pierced blond boy who was a senior. Without a moment's hesitation, this boy swung fiercely at Steven's face. The movement had the swooping athleticism of a very short and brutal dance: Steven fell into him, and the tall, lanky boy stumbled while shifting his weight and, somehow, channeled all his momentum into his fist for a violent, swinging, angry punch that connected squarely with Steven's face. I was so close that I could see a drop of water squirt out of Steven's eye and fling through the space between us in *Matrix*-like bullet-time slow-motion. I felt viscerally the injustice of it—the sheer, aimless hatred, the reality of physical violence being so merciless and awful. A real punch lands in a way that I've still never seen in film or television. It's much quieter, and it hurts more.

That was it. No fight, just an attack that was over before it began. The tall and lanky senior made almost no acknowledgment of what had happened, loping away with a confidence that still chills my blood. In the immediate aftermath, people cleared away like fish do when sharks decide to take one down. Collective powerlessness in the face of brutality. *Keep moving* was the evident rule, which Steven intuited immediately. A few of us crowded around him to make sure he was okay, and he assured us he was. His eye was horribly bloodshot and swollen, but he got up quickly and kept walking. Even now I cringe, not just at the pain inflicted but the unmitigated aggression. It felt wrong, cosmically. Welcome to high school.

From there, it was all downhill for any remaining formal education and me. I would attend Burroughs for less than forty days, a period shorter than Lent. And just like Lent, as of this writing, I still don't really know what high school is like. I'm not saying it doesn't serve a necessary or vital purpose for those who go, but I simply don't know what I missed. I can't remember my classes very well, nor did I forge any lasting friendships during such a brief period. I entered and exited so swiftly that most of my high school memories, outside of that fight on day one, are snapshots barely worth remembering. Instead, the most palpable recollections I have are my feelings at the time. Oh, the feelings. They are much easier to remember than events, and I think they can often be a more truthful reflection of the past. In fact, memories are often rendered so subjectively *by* the feelings surrounding them that, in my attempt to reconstruct any narrative of my high school experience, I have come to regard myself as a wholly unreliable narrator.

Here are the facts: I was short and squat, as a few of my asshole friends would repeatedly remind me. My voice was high and nasally. I had been told that there was something inherently funny about my voice by a professional comedian in a stand-up workshop for teenagers at the Comedy Store, a famous comedy club on Sunset Boulevard. This comic was a woman in her forties who apparently didn't know how to speak to an introverted adolescent, but she wasn't wrong. I would then, as I do now, speak in a monotonous droll when I became self-conscious, and this cracked her up.

Because I was short and squat, I believed my hair was my one shot at appearing tall and thin. When I worked on any TV show or film, I had a minor existential crisis, because every hair stylist on every project had demonstrated that they just couldn't handle curly hair. I don't know what it is about curly hair—there are countless millions of people of nearly every ethnic background with curly hair, right? Somehow, though, no one wants to see it in Hollywood unless it's a reconstructed 1920s-era finger wave on a blond bombshell in a sequined period minidress. Rather than letting my hair be, I learned all about the things my hair couldn't do without a blowout or being flat ironed. I would go into a freeze response every time I sat in a chair in the hair-and-makeup room. I still have to remember to not have this response, even now, as a thirty-eight-year-old man with famously good hair.

What I did with my hair in high school is among the most memorable (and regrettable) things from this very short period of life. Here is my back-to-school-for-the-last-time routine in the fall of 2000: first, still a little damp after a rigorous towel dry, I would do a fast and loose blow-dry with my hands, never a brush. This helped to work out the kinks and curls in a way that still looked natural. After this, I would use a flat iron to straighten all the hair on the front-facing third of my scalp and then apply a very stiff wax, which I also thought looked natural. If you were to place the back of your hand on your forehead and stretch your fingers out as wide as you can, then fan them forward to a sixty-five-degree angle, this would be an accurate rendering of what my hair looked like: natural! It was a genuine surprise to me when someone in my chemistry class called me Duran Duran. I was crestfallen because the boy who said this was an uncharacteristically nice, very popular tenth grader. He typically gave me hope because he was one of the most popular boys in our grade and he was still short, still had a high voice, and he was not gorgeous. Bestie! Then he made fun of my hair in front of two cute girls and everything was called into question. Fucking traitor!

Since I wasn't close with anyone yet, momentary pitfalls like this were cataclysmic shifts in the landscape. I felt alien, like so many do in high school, and the entire time the trap door was calling: *You don't have to go to high school, little Penn.*

Hmm. Interesting.

Dropping out didn't feel like the answer, not at first, because I still cherished the social dimensions of conventional schooling, and I was terrified of not getting a proper education. But after my second week of my sophomore month, the pressures of "real life" were beginning to descend upon me. I was swamped with homework for three hours almost every day, which I had to balance with the afternoon auditions that often came with long commutes in Los Angeles traffic. David E. Kelley shows were the worst, because every audition was in Manhattan Beach, which was effectively a day trip. At least a few times we didn't get home until ten o'clock at night after three or four afternoon auditions all over Los Angeles, so by the time I finished my homework, it was two in the morning. I had to get up in five hours to start my hair routine. My mother knew something about this was unsustainable, and she was right.

One late September evening, dreading my homework, wondering if life might've been easier if I'd started high school as a freshman, I took a swim like it was a smoke break. There was a pool in the courtyard of my apartment complex, and I went down barefoot in the warm twilight. I was submerging myself for as long as I could hold my breath, enjoying the suspension of gravity, of time, and of my chemistry test at the end of the week. I came up out of the water into the balmy air of the southern Californian fall and I looked up at the Disney Channel building poking out over the horizon, glowing like the moon. I listened to the sounds of the freeway, a mechanical rush of speeding cars emitting the constant *whoosh* of a river. Closing my eyes, I had to ask myself, *What do you really want?*

I have trouble answering that question, still, as an adult. At thirteen, the mounting pressure was far too much, and soon the answer came in the form of a job: a recurring role as Phillip Chancellor IV on *The Young and the Restless*. After only a few weeks, my filming schedule became a problem for my attendance at Burroughs. I either needed to quit the job or drop out of school. Conceived only weeks ago, my parachute plan—community college if things start to fall apart—needed execution. I have no memory of what I said to my mom, or the decision-making process, probably because I pulled that rip cord like a wingsuited, BASE-jumping adrenaline junkie with a Red Bull sponsorship. I had already been in a kind of freefall for years that had the sensation, at times, of flight. During those times, it was thrilling. I had no reason to believe it wouldn't keep working.

Had I not been given the opportunity to write a book and reflect on the chances I took from the perspective of a perilous success story—if my career had fizzled instead of flourished in my late teens to midtwenties and I had given my youth to a pursuit that never gave me anything in return; if I had failed—would anyone hesitate to call the same choices my mother and I made *objectively bad*? I don't think so. And yet, those are the choices we made. I don't regret any of them—not because they "worked," or because I don't believe in regret, but because the unconventional circumstances that led my mother and me to this precipice had their origins so much earlier in my life that I can't imagine anything else happening. If there is anything I learned from my unique high school experience, it's from my mother, and her determination to create possibility for me.

To be clear, the auspice under which I got out of high school and took the CHSPE at thirteen years old was a bit of a fudge in the first place—I had taken an online creative writing course that apparently contained *some* college-level curriculum through John Hopkins University, and because this was a program typically for sixteen-year-olds, my mother was able to make the case that I was, academically, sixteen. Name-dropping Johns Hopkins was a lion's share of her tactic, I would imagine.

But my mother was sensible, not crazy. I was doing something unconventional—avoiding high school altogether—as a sensible response to my reality, which was Hollywood. Moving to Hollywood was unconventional, but it was a sensible response to our limited and depressing reality at home in Washington State. Convention, for my family, had led to our collapse. Leaving high school—my mom hates when I say I dropped out—allowed me to embrace the new pattern of life I'd already started years prior. No longer in between worlds, I could fully inhabit one I was choosing rather than one I had to accept. In this Phoenician light, emerging from the ashes of our nuclear family in Washington, going to Los Angeles, and opting out of a formal education is one of the best decisions I've ever made.

And I would never recommend it to anyone else.

What am I supposed to make of my own path that I can't encourage other young actors to follow? I can't promise anyone that they would succeed. They almost certainly wouldn't. It's a statistical anomaly to succeed in Hollywood. To paraphrase Gwen Stefani, herself a statistical anomaly, that shit is bananas. It's not fair. I could, however, encourage them to reorient their focus from *result* to *process*. In my personal attempt to succeed in an unconscionably exclusive industry, the results have been favorable, in part due to sheer luck. The part I could control was the commitment I made to the process, and that I would commend to others. I committed like my life depended on it.

To some degree, it did.

DEVIL WORSHIPPER

NAVA

Being a member of a minority religion isn't all summer camps and washing dishes on Wednesday nights. Once in a while, it's accusations of being in a cult.

Sometimes that happens in a very public way. The one and only time I've ever been referenced on a celebrity gossip account—not by name, but as "Penn Badgley's cohost"—was in 2023, when a debate was unfolding on DeuxMoi about whether or not the Bahá'í Faith was a cult. Our podcast was a tick in the yes column. Apparently, we sounded "culty."*

Other times, it's having your cool teenage neighbor become convinced you worship the devil.

. . .

It's the year 2000. A Friday night, junior year of high school. There's a fireside at my house. A Bahá'í fireside is a gathering where

---

* Referring to Penn as my cult leader is still one of my favorite things to do.

someone, usually a Bahá'í, shares about the principles and teachings of the Bahá'í Faith to a group of people interested in learning more about the religion.

My mom had initiated the Friday night firesides and invited my classmates over the first time herself. We were having a pool party, and during dinner a kid asked my dad a question about whether Bahá'ís could own guns. This turned into an hour-long conversation led mostly by my parents, and by the end of it, my mom had proclaimed that every Friday night we would open our apartment to anyone who wanted to learn more about the Bahá'í Faith.

I had mixed feelings about this invitation.

On one hand, I was a hardcore Bahá'í. As a small religion with lofty goals like "establish world peace," we do, in fact, wish to grow, and people need to learn about the religion for growth to occur.

On the other hand, I was a teenager who wanted her friends not to think of her as a weirdo.

In the end, my inner, hardcore Bahá'í won out, and I even thanked my mom for coming up with the idea.

So back to Friday night. This particular fireside is being led by the beautiful Jamal Peters, a fellow Bahá'í and college medical school student who could have been Jared Leto's stand-in (in his Jordan Catalano/*My So-Called Life* era). Jamal is the most beautiful teenage boy I've ever seen in real life, and many of my friends feel the same way. Jamal has been attending firesides sporadically with his Catholic girlfriend so she can better understand him, and it's not long before word spreads that Nava is friends with the most beautiful boy alive. The most beautiful, *older* boy alive. Tonight he's facilitating a conversation about the core tenets of the Bahá'í Faith. The house has never been more packed. I'm sure teenage interest in the Bahá'í Faith is at a fever pitch, and Jamal's movie-star good looks are irrelevant.

If I recall correctly, it was my staunchest Christian friend, who ordinarily skipped Friday Firesides, who pitched the idea of Jamal leading a conversation about the Bahá'í Faith. "I'd love a refresher, and Jamal seems so smart," she offered the week before.

Apart from the awe and wonder provided by Jamal's piercing green eyes and strong oratory skills, this night is particularly special because, for the first time ever, I've invited one of my neighbors over. Cassandra is a gorgeous Argentinian girl who moved into the building just the month before. She invited me to the beach earlier in the week, and we'd spent a surprising amount of time talking about personal faith.

Cassandra is Catholic.

I tell her I'm Bahá'í, and when she asks me what that means, I summon the courage to invite her to the fireside. Do I tremble for a few minutes wondering if this cool-girl-whose-approval-I'm-already-desperate-for might reject me? Sure. But I do it anyway. That's called growth. And Cassandra accepts my invitation with real enthusiasm! Nothing could possibly go wrong.

When Cassandra enters the apartment, ten minutes into the presentation, there's a discernible shift in the room. Everyone else already knows each other—we're either all classmates at the Episcopal Cathedral School or we've attended at least one other fireside. So when gorgeous, mysterious Cassandra enters the room, all the boys sit up a little straighter, Diego included. (Refresher: Diego = my ardent crush.) All the girls take note.

Jamal gives a stunning presentation . . . or his stunning-ness amplifies the presentation. Either way, the vibes are A+.

Everyone is happy. The atmosphere is curious.

Maybe my different religion can be one of the cool things about me, I start to muse for the first time in my life.

We then enter the Questions and Answers portion of the evening.

Cassandra raises her hand. She asks, in Spanish, *"En quien creen ustedes? Dios?"* ("Who do you [all] believe in? God?")

Cassandra's late arrival means she missed the very first point Jamal made, which is that Baháʼís believe in an All-Loving Creator, aka God.

Jamal responds, *"El Diablo."*

The Devil.

I wait for him to laugh. He doesn't.

This is particularly perplexing because in addition to the fact that Baháʼís do *not* worship the devil, the Baháʼí Faith may hold the distinction of being the first religion to go on record stating that the devil is a construct, and the only "devil" to fear is the ego within. This may seem par for the course now, but in the nineties, most of my Christian friends *did* believe in the devil. So not believing in the devil was another idea that made me different. Needless to say: we are 100 percent a non-devil-worshipping religion.

I look at Jamal again, with a face that indicates confused betrayal.

Then I glance over at Cassandra, whose face is lit with horror. She's already halfway up from her chair, ready to escape the clutches of this group of sixteen-year-old devil worshippers she's been tricked into joining. A bath in holy water will follow, I assume.

Diego, Catholic, is the first to laugh. *"Mano, no! Ella dijo Dios!"* ("No, dude, she said God!")

Diego, unburdened by the tremendous anxiety of being accepted by a pretty, cool girl despite a "weird" religion, has immediately understood what happened.

Jamal *heard* the question as *"En quién creen ustedes? El diablo?"* and responded by repeating what he thought he heard, "El diablo?" *question mark*, not "El diablo" period. He was trying to clarify her question, not answer it.

Jamal bursts out laughing. He manages to eke out, *"¡No! ¡No! ¡Creemos en Dios!"* ("No! No! We believe in God!") and soon the whole room is laughing. Even Cassandra is laughing. At this point, she sits back down and stays for the rest of the conversation.

Is she a little on edge, though? I wonder. I don't know her well enough yet to understand the default vibes. I'm probably imagining it.

Cassandra and I are gonna be cool, I tell myself. *We're gonna be friends. My best friend is going to live in my building! My best friend and I are going to laugh about that time Jamal told her I worship the devil!*

Welp. That was the first and last time Cassandra ever came over to my apartment. Incidentally, she never invited me to the beach, or anywhere else, again.

IN HER ORBIT

SOPHIE

As soon as the bell rang to signal the end of the day, Siria made her way down the hall, through the after-school rush, and toward the gymnasium. She found the paper taped to the wall that read "JUNIOR VARSITY TRACK AND FIELD." Her eyes darted around the list, scanning the names.

My older sister, Siria, was not the most athletic student; she wasn't even the most athletic family member (congratulations, Kalan, that one goes to you), but in 2007 she decided she wanted to give sports a shot. A handful of her friends ran track and field, and in her sophomore year she set her sights on joining them. If she could make it to the team, it would buy her a significant amount of social capital at school. By a dash of determination and a stroke of luck, she did it. She found her name in twelve-point font on the flimsy sheet of paper flapping in the wind, outside the gymnasium.

At family gatherings now, my brother often retells the story of the first time he watched Siria in a track meet. It was the 100-meter hurdles, and while the rest of the runners had their heads forward, game faces on, Siria was trailing well behind, with a big, goofy grin on her face. Kalan says that that was the precise moment he knew that Siria was destined for intramural sports.

Siria excelled at many things, but she was exceptionally proud to have made it on the track team. She had a corkboard on her bedroom door where she tacked her favorite photos of her and her friends, magazine cutouts of cute actors, and bold text that spoke to her. She would switch things out regularly, depending on her interests and how she was feeling. It was one of the ways she expressed herself, a manifestation of her mind and heart for all to see. She came home from the track meet that day, goofy smile still on her face, and she pinned her number on the corkboard. Front and center. You knew what was deeply important to my sister by what she placed on that corkboard, which is why I am ashamed to tell you what I did next.

A couple weeks after the track meet, I was doing my duty as little sister, annoying her to no end. All I wanted was to be close to her. On this particular day, I was begging her to let me in her room after she had locked me out. She's three years older than me, but her room was at least a couple decades cooler than mine. I still had a butterfly bedspread with stuffed toys lined up on top. She had a stereo in her room where she could play her own music, and even though it was light and airy, to me it felt like a nightclub. I banged on the door, screaming for her to let me in. She just turned up the music to drown me out. I could hear Kings of Leon getting louder and louder, seeping through the crack between the door and the frame.

There was no hope of breaking through the noise. Eventually, I stopped banging, realizing it was futile. I was exasperated and bored, a lethal combination. I started plotting other ways of getting my sister's attention. I could slip a note under her door, but she would just ignore it. I could tell my mom on her, but she hadn't done anything tattle worthy. None of my usual tactics were standing out to me.

My mind started to wander, and I perused her latest corkboard configuration. Her track number was taking up most of the board at the moment. She loved what that number symbolized: accomplishment, hard work, and social standing. Before I even had a chance to think it through, scissors materialized in my hand and I sliced the number in half.

A wave of guilt immediately washed over me.

Maybe I can staple it back together? Maybe Kalan has an old one that I can switch out? Maybe she won't care?

But I knew she would.

I panicked, but I had enough sense to leave the scene of the crime before I was caught with the scissors in my hand. I tried to make myself busy so I could forget what I did, but after an hour or so of futzing around in my bedroom, behind the safety of a locked door, I heard a bloodcurdling scream. Now Siria was the one banging on my door. She demanded that I face her. She was livid, but she was also clearly holding back tears. Seeing my normally bossy, confident older sister hurt in that way really stung. Even though I felt ashamed, outwardly all I did was defend myself and whine about how it was basically her fault for not letting me in her room in the first place.

This wasn't the first time that adoration turned into obsession and then into rage for not getting the attention I sought from her. Ever since I could remember, I had followed my sister around like a puppy dog—lapping at her feet, taking any time she would give me.

• • •

Once we moved to Beijing, we began to build a more reciprocal friendship. I was in the middle of eighth grade when we arrived in China, and Siria was in eleventh. Although we were both attending the Western Academy of Beijing (WAB), our campuses were separated by a small river. It took about ten minutes to walk over the bridge that connected the middle and high schools.

Shortly after we arrived, the Bahá'í month of fasting began. During the fast, Bahá'ís between the ages of fifteen and seventy refrain from eating and drinking from sunrise to sunset for the duration of the month of Alá,* which falls inside of March. Siria had just turned seventeen, and as had been the case in all our schools, we were the only Bahá'ís at WAB. I was still too young to fast, and Kalan was already in college, which meant Siria was the only person in the entire school who wasn't eating lunch.

To avoid the temptation of food while her friends ate, she ventured across the bridge to the middle school to spend her lunch hour with me. High schoolers *never* graced the middle school with their presence, especially not by choice. The lounge where we ate our lunch had an entirely glass wall that gave me and my new friends a perfect view of the path from the high school campus. The image of Siria walking across the bridge to come and hang out with me on the first day of the fast is burned into my memory. She wore a green

---

* The Bahá'í calendar is made up of nineteen months, each with nineteen days, and four to five intercalary days. Each month is named after an attribute of God. *Alá* is the Arabic word for "loftiness."

miniskirt with black tights and Uggs. Peak 2008. All my friends were fawning over her, just as honored as I was that a junior was joining us for lunch. She came every day for the rest of the week. The fact that Siria came to spend time with me, her nobody-baby-sister, made me feel rich in the truest sense of the word.

• • •

Once Siria left the house for college, our friendship *really* blossomed. It's amazing how close two sisters can get when the opportunity to vandalize personal property is removed.

When I started college the summer of 2013, she had just graduated from her musical theater program at the Boston Conservatory, and we both moved to New York City in the sweaty August heat. This was the first time since I was fifteen that we lived in the same vicinity. But now the tables had turned. I was no longer an angsty high schooler, and now *Siria* was desperate to spend time with *me*. Our text history was filled with blue bubbles of her asking where I was, could we hang out, why wasn't I answering? We had different interests and different priorities, and I didn't go out of my way to carve out time for her. Outside of our brief stint living together for six months in NYC, we would meet for coffee when I had a free hour, dinner *occasionally*, or bump into each other at Bahá'í community events. Siria would run to me, we'd cuddle and giggle, and then I'd inevitably leave her to talk to a friend. Siria was perpetually chasing me. Looking back, I wish I had slowed down.

A couple Augusts later, she got an acting gig that took her to Scotland for the Edinburgh Fringe Festival. She met a boy there who was in medical school at the University of Edinburgh. She swore he was just a friend, but after she landed back in New York, they both realized it was more. He was endgame. Siria's days in the city were numbered, and they went by fast. A few visits between them, and the next thing I knew, I was helping her box up her things and preparing for a new brother-in-law to join the family. The weight of time wasted started to settle on me.

All I wanted as a kid was to be in my big sister's orbit, and all Siria wanted in our early twenties was my approval and proximity. Neither one of us could give the other what they wanted at the time, but I'm relieved to say that our circling has finally converged.

As adults, we try to see each other as much as we can, but it involves arduous journeys with multiple legs and long-haul flights, so it ends up being once or twice a year at most. When we do reunite, we melt into each other. Holding Siria's hand feels like holding my own hand. Her body is an extension of mine. I've never felt that way with anyone else, not even my own husband. My friends who have seen us together say it's like we're intertwined.

As wrapped up in each other as we are, I still feel like I'm trying to catch up to Siria sometimes. Just six months after my sister became a mother, we shared a bed together on a family trip. Siria and I had shared many beds in the past, but this time we contorted our bodies to make space between us for her new baby, Theodora. Postpartum is a particularly intimate and vulnerable time. My sister was coping remarkably well for a new mom traveling alone with a baby, but I knew she was struggling. I woke up one night to a deep yell. It took a second for me to get my bearings and realize what was happening. Theodora had woken for the umpteenth time that night, and Siria had reached her limit. But, as many moms will understand, reaching her limit was simply not an option, so she hastily picked up Theo to begin rocking her back to sleep.

"Siria, be careful; she's just a baby," I whispered. There was an undeniable judgment in my voice.

Siria was sitting on the edge of the bed now, with her back to me. She never responded. I had no idea what my sister was going through at the time, but I think I do now. Just last week I was struggling to get my own baby to nap after a tough morning. I was overstimulated and just trying to tune out her screams so I could keep myself calm. When I walked into our room to put her down in the bed, I saw the pile of laundry that I had asked my husband, David, to put away before he left for the studio. I needed to move it to use the bed, but with a writhing baby in my arms, I couldn't. A simple mistake that shouldn't have mattered, but my entire body tensed, and I let out a long, stifled scream. A guttural, primal reaction. Four years later, I understood exactly what had happened in the half light that night on vacation. I can't count how many times I have gone to Siria to vent about this type of experience in motherhood. Like many older sisters before her, she quietly went through the fire, just to turn around and extend her hand to me. She has never made me feel bad for not being there when she needed a hand herself.

I wish everyone could be her little sister. Siria is my sounding board, my confidant, and my very best friend. I won't soon forget the years that we lost, but I am doing my best to make up for them.

THE MIDDLE

NAVA

Bleed American, the fourth studio album by American rock band Jimmy Eat World, is etched into my memories as the soundtrack of my sweetest year. It came out just after my seventeenth birthday, right in the thick of summer, just before my senior year of high school. Jimmy Eat World wasn't just a band; they were a heartbeat. The album's title track, "The Middle," became my anthem—a promise that I was only in the bumpy middle of my life, that the best was yet to come. I played that song so often that I literally scratched the CD. Sometimes I'd hop onto my bed and scream about being in the middle of the ride at the top of my lungs and then crash back down, letting Jim Adkins* comfort me with a promise that everything would be alright. I would lie on my bed, fantasizing about a time that I might feel fully confident in myself. At seventeen, unlike the kids in the song's music video, I wasn't a cool teenager going to house parties in my underwear. I'd never

---

* The lead vocalist of Jimmy Eat World.

made out with someone in a refrigerator; in fact, I'd never made out with anyone at all. Still. "The Middle" gave me hope that my day was coming.

And for one month during the summer of my seventeenth spin around the sun, I felt *legitimately* cool. I understood what it meant to feel like the world was your oyster. Because for one month I got to spend every day with Ariana Karamallis: the bohemian-chic writer, poet, unlikely-best-friend I'd made from the United States.

Ariana and I met during our freshman year of high school at a summer program called the Badasht Academy, at Green Acre. She was from Jersey, spending weekends in New York City. I was from Puerto Rico, spending weekends in my apartment. When we got assigned as roommates at Green Acre, I remember thinking, *There's no way we're going to be friends.* She was striking, with wild curls, sharp green eyes, and effortless, athletic grace. I just couldn't picture us talking about anything. Then, a couple of days into camp, she got appendicitis and was rushed to the hospital. When it was clear she wouldn't be well enough to return, her younger sister, Zandy, took her spot. (Decades later, Zandy and I became close friends when we ended up living a few blocks away from each other in Brooklyn.) A few weeks later, I was back in Puerto Rico, sophomore year just getting started. I was on AOL Instant Messenger when a message popped up onscreen.

Sunshinecurlz: Hi Nava! It's Ariana!

NavainPR: Ariana from Green Acre?

Sunshinecurlz: Yah! I got your SN from Zandy.

My stomach flipped. Ariana had gotten my screen name from her sister? She had gone out of her way to find me? We started talking every day, like it was the most natural thing in the world. I didn't even realize it was happening until we were deep into sharing everything—our writing, our thoughts, our nothing-has-ever-mattered-more high school dramas. I still remember the first poem she sent me. It was written from the perspective of soldiers in the Vietnam War. I sat there staring at my screen in awe. *Who writes like this?* She was writing poetry that felt too big for us—like she had a world of experience I couldn't touch. Until that point, I had only written poems about unrequited love. After reading Ariana's poetry, I tried to write about "things that mattered," but the results were . . . less than great. (I think I wrote a poem about capitalism, which I peripherally understood was "bad," but didn't actually understand at all. I think one of the verses was *"We toil in labor / In wages we're paid / But for wages we toil / And in labor we fade."*)

Ariana was simply the coolest girl I'd ever met. She was confident, assertive, and when she liked someone, she just *said it*. She slipped into relationships with ease. Me? I'd never admitted to someone I liked them. Ariana's family was wealthier than mine and her clothes cuter. Prior to meeting Ariana, I'd feel anxious in every interaction with someone I thought was cooler than me, desperate to prove I was interesting, too. I deserved to be their friend! But I never felt that way with Ari. Even though I constantly wondered why she liked me, I was always myself around her. She knew everything I *hadn't* done with boys, my love of pop music (I was stunned to learn she also listened to Britney sometimes), and how deeply insecure I felt around the girls at school. She was the first friend I could show every part of myself to—the parts I liked, the parts I didn't, and the parts I wanted to become.

The unfolding of my friendship with Ariana felt like casting a spell as a joke and learning that I was secretly a witch.

One day, as sophomore year was wrapping up, Ariana and I were chatting about our summer plans.

NavainPR: Ari, you should come visit me in Puerto Rico!

It was something I said casually. I wanted her to come; it just didn't occur to me she might.

Sunshinecurlz: OMG, I would love that! I'll ask my parents.

No, I thought when I saw her immediate response. *She's* tāroffing.*

The next day I was at my desk at four p.m. Sunshinecurlz logged on.

Sunshinecurlz: We have a family trip to Greece in August, but my parents said I could come in July. I'm thinking of booking a flight from July 14–August 2. Would that work?

First feeling: shock. *Ariana Karamallis* is going to be the first person to ever visit me from another country?!

Second feeling: fear. *Oh crap. I need to ask my parents if this is okay!*

---

* *Tārof* (تعارف) is a Persian cultural concept that refers to a complex system of social etiquette, politeness, and deference in interactions. It involves offering things out of courtesy (such as food, compliments, or help) even when you don't necessarily mean it.

A few weeks later my mom and I drove to the airport in Carolina to pick her up. I was nervous the entire drive. What if our apartment was too small? What if Puerto Rico was too humid? What if my mom wasn't cool enough? I loved my mom, but she was definitely not a "cool" mom. But the second Ari walked into our place, all that worry melted away. She got along with my family, my friends, and somehow even seemed to enjoy the sticky heat of Puerto Rican summers.

We bought matching tankinis (RIP the tankini) at the mall, and she squealed in delight when she found a pair of Rainbow flip-flops on sale at the neighborhood Quicksilver. We stayed up late into the night talking about God and religion. We both loved Tahirih, the fearless Persian poetess and martyr who tore off her veil and declared that it was time for the emancipation of women. We encouraged each other's highest aspirations and held space for each other's greatest insecurities. During her visit, we took a short trip to the Dominican Republic to participate in a Bahá'í Youth Conference, and Ariana was even chiller than I was about the stripped-down accommodations, broken showers (to this day, that trip holds the record for my longest shower-free streak: seven days), and the tarantulas that crawled the grounds (where I was terrified, her sense of adventure tickled). I was an unbelievably picky eater back then, and did not yet have the grace to try to bend to the local culture. Ariana did. She ate most of the meals without complaining and lost five pounds. I subsisted only on bread and gained three. *Of course.*

Ariana fell in love with a Puerto Rican Bahá'í, which drew us even closer together. My friend group had included a boy she deemed worthy of dating. I was proud.

The next summer Ariana invited me into her world, and I got to experience Morristown, New Jersey, and the richness of her very different lifestyle. Ariana's parents were incredible. I felt like their third daughter (a feeling that remains to this day), and I instantly adored them. That summer was magical.

We took art classes in New York City and had lunch with boys who were Princeton bound. We went to parties in basements where, sober, I still felt like I fit in. I'd never actually spent a full month in the United States, with American kids. I realized part of what made that trip so special was that I was feeling a little more culturally at ease. While I loved Puerto Rico, it always felt like a second home. The United States was first, and that summer helped me accept that.

In the middle of my and Ari's month together, we drove from New Jersey to Maine for another summer at Green Acre, holding hands along the way, listening to the curated CDs we'd each burned for the road trip. Ariana played hers first. The first song was "The Middle" off *Bleed American*. I squealed. "Wait! Ari, oh my God! Can I play my mix for a second?"

"Sure!" she replied. We popped her CD out and put mine in.

My first song was also "The Middle." We burst out laughing and squeezed each other's hands. This was the first time we'd chosen the same song (and the same *opening song*!) on our CDs. It felt like the best omen. Like somehow everything was going to be just right. We spent the car ride giggling about the boys we were most excited to see again at our final year of Badasht. (Her Puerto Rican adventure had fizzled out by then.) We talked about our college aspirations. By the end of the drive, we'd made a pact to both apply to Smith College in Massachusetts, our future laid out like a treasure map.

It almost felt like fate when we both got in. But Smith didn't offer me a very big scholarship, and my parents strongly advised me against taking out loans to pay for college. I planned on becoming an English teacher; why would I start my life in serious debt? I let rationality win over emotion and went to a university in Texas because it offered me the best financial package. I don't remember how I broke the news to Ariana, but I remember occasionally wondering if she felt a little betrayed by my choice. Neither of us ever acknowledged the disappointment of our dream dying.

Over the next few years we stayed in touch through emails and care packages, each visiting the other once during our university tenure. Over time, our lives drifted in different directions and, perhaps predictably, we lost the closeness we once had.

Ariana and I are occasionally in touch now, though it's never been like it was when we were seventeen. But no matter how many friends I've made or will make, there will only be one Ari: a friend who let me copy her and pretended not to notice, a friend who healed some of my deepest insecurities simply by witnessing me, a friend who actually *was* too cool for me but loved me so intensely I never felt jealous—only seen, only chosen. Even as time stretched the distance between us, I carried her with me—imprinted to this day in my taste of music, of poetry, in the Rainbow flip-flops I wear religiously when the weather tips above seventy-eight degrees.

Every time I hear "The Middle," the first thing I think of is me and Ari, driving up the I-95, holding hands, believing that the best of our story was still to come.

LOVE FROM BROOKLYN

SOPHIE

All of my childhood memories are sorted by place. When I pluck a particular memory from the recesses of my mind, I see a mini Sophie rifling through filing cabinets. Each cabinet is labeled with a location, and each drawer and individual file becomes geographically more specific. I know that my first memory is from the age of two, because it was in our home in Pakistan. I know that I was between the ages of six and eight when we lost our dog, Chloe, because we were living in Albania at the time. The video about invertebrates that I made with my dad for a school project featured our yard in Rome, so that had to be third grade. You get the idea.

I've lived in the same country for over a decade now, but place is still one of my main markers for time. I imagine a person who has spent their entire childhood in the same country, the same town, the same home, even, might have other ways to distinguish the timing of their memories. I know I have, at various times, used seasons, friendships, and exes to parse out my experiences and pinpoint them on a timeline. Still, place has remained my main marker.

In the seven years that I called New York my home, I lived in six different apartments. Each home saw a new version of me. Six different flats, six different lives. If I call to mind a particular address, I am transported back to a very singular time in my life.

35 FIFTH AVENUE
NEW YORK, NEW YORK

My first landing pad was in Manhattan, just north of Washington Square Park, with probably the swankiest address I'll *ever* have—although the living quarters were not quite as luxe. I spent one year at 35 Fifth Avenue, where I slept on the fifteenth floor of Rubin Hall, the only NYU dorm without air-conditioning. I lived in a suite and shared a moldy bathroom with three other girls.

There was my roommate, Katy, whose family was half Chinese and half Filipino. When I tried to bond over our shared connections to China and the Philippines—where I had lived for a combined decade—Katy was at best uninterested, and at worst offended. She was a California girl through and through. In the adjoining room was Kylie, a musical theater major from New Jersey who left the city for days at a time to do laundry on the other side of the Holland Tunnel. Her roommate, Camille, was sunshine and sugar incarnate. She grew up in a small town in France, and coming to NYU was the culmination of her lifelong obsession with the city.

I was also new to living in the USA, so Camille and I banded together as the two *not-quite-American* suitemates. When I think of Camille, I picture her with her arms outstretched, twirling in Central Park. She understood that there was magic in every moment that we were there. I could have learned a thing or two from Camille. I thought I had no time for twirling. I had always been in a rush to grow up and move on to the next phase of life, and that was true of my time in college, too. I had taken a gap year between high school and university and I thought that made me too mature to waste time socializing with the rest of the freshmen—a foolishly *immature* thought.

I wound up treating my first year at NYU like a job, stopping in for classes and finding community elsewhere. I threw myself into my Bahá'í service. I spent many afternoons and weekends with a group of middle schoolers—playing games, reading stories, and engaging in art activities—all with the aim of helping them direct their energy toward service to their community. As soon as I was no longer required to be in campus housing at the end of freshman year, I moved closer to the families I worked with on the Lower East Side. That was when I began to feel like a *real* adult.

540 EAST TWENTIETH ST.
NEW YORK, NEW YORK

I was confronted with the reality of post-dorm life when I moved into a one-bed/one-bath apartment just off the East River with my sister and her best friend from college. I know what you're thinking—but yes, with an active imagination and some elbow grease, it *is* possible for three girls to live in a one-bedroom apartment. My sister, Siria, and I took it back to our roots to share the only room with a door. We crammed two dressers and two beds into the room, and when we were done, there was almost no space to walk. Our beds were so close we could have probably touched toes in our sleep.

Our third roommate crafted a makeshift bedroom in the living area, using a curtain rod and some creativity. Our common space was left with no natural light, but when I look back on that brief period, I have fond memories. Living with my sister and her best friend, Ashley, while they navigated New York City as recent graduates scratched my obsessed-with-adulthood itch. Siria and Ashley had just completed four years of a musical theater program, so they spent their days running between auditions and their nights working as servers in restaurants. I thought that was so quintessentially New York. I ran lines with my sister on the couch in the evenings to help her prepare for the next day's auditions, and we giggled at my lack of acting chops. We helped each other; I humored her by singing all the duets she wanted, and she cooked me heaping bowls of spaghetti. When our days off overlapped, we hopped around the city together. Siria showed me new coffee shops, and I swiped her into the college cafeteria for free meals at our dad's expense. But our priorities soon began to veer from one another.

After volunteering at the Bahá'í gardens, I was feeling more firm in my faith than ever, and I can now admit that I was overly zealous. I would do obnoxious things, like ask my sister if she had said her prayers that day, as if I was some moral authority. I was eager to host discussion nights at our apartment, so I could invite college friends into meaningful conversations about things like service, prayer, and purpose. Siria was also keen, but understandably hesitant—we had a third roommate who literally slept in our living space, and she didn't want to impose on her. I get it now, but at the time I felt stifled. I had little time for anything other than community service, and when Siria wanted to hang out, I was almost always "too busy" to oblige.

I started spending more and more time in Brooklyn, with a crew of Bahá'í youth who hosted a devotional gathering at their home every Friday night. In fact, one of the girls who lived in the home, Shirin, had been my sister's friend first. Shirin and I grew close quickly, and soon our friendship overtook that of her and Siria's. Suddenly I was spending more time on the C train to Bed-Stuy than I was with my sister.

Siria never confronted me about the way that I left her hanging, but I later found out that she would cry to our mom on the phone. She felt lonely.

When I go through my memories of our life on East Twentieth Street, I conveniently skip over the near-constant sisterly arguments that led to me moving out after just six months. It's difficult for me to face how callous I was, and the lack of care that I had for Siria in those final months of living together makes my insides churn. I gave up living with my favorite person, all because of some stupid fights and misaligned priorities. That was the last time we would live under one roof, and I would give anything to be able to go back and relive those six months. But when a potential spot opened in Shirin's house, I saw it as an opportunity, and I brusquely packed up my possessions.

When I stepped out of the subway station on Franklin Avenue, I was relieved to have some personal space, and non-relative roommates. Although I was still a sophomore in college and living off a stipend from my father, I felt like I was finally out on my own as I had left the dorms and my family behind.

PUTNAM AVE.
BROOKLYN, NEW YORK

I left the bustle of Manhattan in a huff and moved into a two-bedroom house with Shirin and Taraneh, who would turn out to become lifelong friends. The two bedrooms in the house were already spoken for, so I made a cozy nook out of the boiler room under the stairs. When I went to measure the space, we found an open flame under the boiler. *No worries*, I thought, *I'll just buy a carbon monoxide detector*. Problem solved.

On my first night in the house, I prepared my bed as cute as I could, but there was no way around it: the boiler room was depressing. Shirin knew it, too. She swooped in as I was slipping the last pillowcase on and suggested I sleep in her room. "Just for tonight," she said.

Despite the neatly made bed, I never did sleep in the room under the stairs. I spent the next eight months sharing Shirin's queen bed. Our physical closeness mirrored the emotional intimacy that developed between us. "Best friend" isn't an adequate term to describe who she is to me now.

Shirin became my surrogate older sister on Putnam Avenue, but unlike my actual sister, she was blunt in a way that encouraged me to grow up. The fifth time I used her nail clippers, she gently asked, "Do you have your own nail clippers?" My shoulders dropped.

"Oh, uhh, no, I don't," I responded.

"What did you use before you moved in?"

I paused. "My sister's."

Similar exchanges took place over face wash, nail polish remover, tweezers, and many other items until I realized two things:

1. It was time to build my own collection of toiletries.
2. Siria had been quietly, diligently taking care of me. Not only did she let me use all her things when we lived together, but she cooked for me, gave me Midol when I got cramps, and generally filled in many of the gaps where I hadn't quite learned how to take care of myself yet. It took moving out to realize how she had cradled me so comfortably.

My time overlapping with Shirin on Putnam Avenue was short but concentrated. After less than a year in the house, Shirin fell in love with a six-foot-four Canadian boy who penned love songs for her on her birthday and adored her in the way she deserved. She moved out when they decided to marry, and we all cried. It was the end of something truly special.

On Putnam Avenue, I learned how much growing up I still had to do, and I began to find a balance between service and the other parts of my life. Shirin, Taraneh, and I taught virtues classes for children in the neighborhood, planned service projects, and generally made efforts to bring our neighbors together, but we also spent hours every week watching *The Walking Dead* and going out for maple lattes.

We loved our little home on Putnam Avenue in Brooklyn . . . but so did the rats. Taraneh and I continued living there after Shirin left. Surprisingly, the night we found fourteen baby rodents in various parts of the kitchen was not the nail in the coffin of our time there. We learned to live among the critters until something died in the walls. It left a foul smell wafting throughout the whole house, so when our crooked landlord told us to simply "wait until it decomposes," we flexed our tenant rights and broke our lease. Every few months we would walk past the house to see what had become of it, but no one moved back in. I imagine it still makes a luxurious home for its four-legged residents.

126 JEFFERSON ST.
BROOKLYN, NEW YORK

Just a few blocks away from Rat Palace, Taraneh and I found a newly renovated flat and moved in with a new roommate, Jaspar. Taraneh and Jaspar's friendship went way back, but I slipped right into the dynamic without a hitch. We spent almost every evening sprawled across the couches in our living room chatting about boys, dogs, and the purpose of life. We hosted countless community gatherings, watched an obscene amount of reality TV, and ate our weight in bodega snacks. For the second time, Taraneh and I had stumbled into an exceptional living situation. The three of us still have an active group chat together today (it's called "dogz").

A lot changed in the year and a half that I lived on Jefferson. I found the "Cheap and Cheerful" section of Jamie Oliver's recipe website and finally started cooking for myself. I graduated from college with a degree in childhood education and special education. I got engaged to my husband, David! (You'll learn more about him in the next essay.) I started working my first big-girl job as a fifth-grade teacher. And my parents kicked me off the family phone plan, which was the surest sign of my transition from kid to adult. It's safe to say that by this point, my toiletry bag was stocked with supplies that I bought myself.

The only thing that could have torn me from my roommates at good ol' 126 Jeff was the love of my life . . . and when he agreed to move to New York City, I started apartment hunting.

418 QUINCY ST.
BROOKLYN, NEW YORK

David and I waded through a lot of crappy online listings in search of a place to live before he touched down. When my mom was in town, she joined my hunt on the ground. We met a real estate agent in a dark hallway of a nondescript building. She opened the door and the three of us stared in silence. There was a pile of dirt, two feet tall, right in the middle of the living room. We turned to her, and before we could even ask, she sighed and said, "I don't know," on the exhale. Something told me this wasn't the most bizarre thing she'd seen in her years as a New York City real estate agent.

We continued scouring StreetEasy and Zillow and eventually found a diamond in the rough, a quaint two-bedroom tucked away in a far corner of Bed-Stuy. There was barely any natural light and the bedrooms' already low ceilings slanted even lower by the tiny windows, but it didn't have mold, or a boiler burning an eternal flame, or a decaying animal in the walls, or a pile of dirt in the living room. For us, it was perfect.

The attic apartment took me just outside the radius of my

close-knit crew of friends, who all lived within a few blocks of one another on the other end of Bed-Stuy. Between the urge for David and me to cocoon as newlyweds in our own little pod and the inconvenient distance, this marked the beginning of a period of relative separation from my friends. The previous four years had revolved so much around my friendships, so the isolation felt disorienting. But David could use the second bedroom as a music studio and there was a cute café around the corner, so we made it work.

There will always be a tiny space in my heart carved out especially for our little home at the tippy top of that brick building. But when David found a recording studio space a few miles away in the Brooklyn Navy Yard, we knew it was time to climb down from the attic and downsize.

511 MONROE ST.
BROOKLYN, NEW YORK

Our final home in New York was hands down the most beautiful. It didn't matter that it was a seventeen-minute walk to the nearest subway because David, like a true suburban boy, had insisted on having a car in New York City. In the summer of 2018, when we still lived in the attic apartment, we took ten days and drove his old 2001 Volvo from Seattle to New York, only to rack up parking tickets every week when it sat on the wrong side of the block due to New York City's Alternate Side Parking for street sweeping regulations. Two monthly subway cards probably would have been cheaper in the long run.

This move took us deeper into Bed-Stuy and even farther from my circle of friends. There was, at most, a twenty-three-minute walk between our home on Monroe and all of my friends on the other side of Marcus Garvey Boulevard, but at the time it felt like an ocean.

In our time on Monroe Street I was drowning in my job as a teacher: I woke up at five and worked until ten most days, and somehow I was always falling behind. Between trying to keep up at work and tending to my still-new relationship with David, my commitments to service were slipping. I was missing meetings, canceling children's classes, and ducking out early from community gatherings. Across the ocean, my sister had found her stride and was flourishing in her service in Scotland. We had flip-flopped, except when I told her of my struggles, she never made me feel small.

When I'd moved from Manhattan to Brooklyn, I'd been so excited about living with friends that I'd failed to recognize it was also the last time I would live with my sister. In the same way, my giddiness over living with a partner for the first time eclipsed the fact that the era of living with my girlfriends was over.

The physical distance that gradually grew between me and my friends with each move marked the end of a very particular phase in my life.

1172 N ARDMORE AVE.
LOS ANGELES, CALIFORNIA

In May of 2020, we packed up our life on Monroe Street, this time for a move farther afield to sunny Los Angeles. Whenever I tell anyone the date of our move, there is a sharp intake of breath that follows. We may all have different markers for time in our lives, but there is one we all share, and that is the spring of 2020. I can pretty much guarantee that you know where you were on March 13 of that year. I turned twenty-six on March 13, 2020, but it feels like the day that marks the end of my youth. The rest of my twenties zoomed by in a series of vignettes of married life, the transition to self-employment, and seasonless LA sun, but the first half feels twice as long and is neatly contained in New York.

I knew I'd be sad to leave New York *whenever* it happened, but it felt especially piercing to leave when we did. New York was not herself. Most of the year it can feel like a real chore to live in the city. Trash in the streets, rats in your home, and blistering cold walks to the train. You endure a lot just to get by, but you endure it for the sake of the month of May. The blossoms are out, the weather is turning; it's the Brooklyn you see in the movies. In the weeks before our departure, there were still blossoms and it was warming up right on cue, but leaving a shuttered city in the height of a global pandemic felt like saying goodbye to a loved one when they're sick.

Of course, we were desperately missing the pizza from Paulie Gee's and sitting on the pier at Transmitter Park, but what I really longed for was my community: the people who had seen me through the roller coaster of my early twenties, helped us nurture our young marriage, and showed us what it looks like to lovingly be of service to the people around us. Leaving when the streets were quiet and everyone was huddled inside robbed me of a proper goodbye.

Just like all the countries I'd lived in as a child and a teen, New York is now a portal. It is a physical place that can pull me back into the emotions of my early twenties.

I have gone back to New York many times in the years since we left, and I have loved it on every trip. But we have both changed, the city and me, and it will never be the New York of my early twenties again. New York is evolving all the time, gathering the stories of all its inhabitants like new wallpaper plastered on top of old by each successive tenant.

The City belongs to no one, but there is a secret version of it that exists just for me. I can step into a certain subway station, pass a specific brownstone, or round a particular corner and be smacked in the face by a sense memory so vivid it feels current. All I have to do is walk the streets around Washington Square Park, Bedford Avenue, or the Nostrand Avenue A/C subway stop, and I'm back in the 2010s, laughing and crying my way through early adulthood with my sister, my girlfriends, or my new husband. It turns out that time travel is possible—I just have to touch down at JFK airport and I'm whooshed right back.

LOS(S)

NAVA

My best friend in middle school was a boy named Luis Oscar Sanchez.

We were classmates who became close in fifth grade, and he was my sweetest friend during the most insecure period of my life. Luis was gay at a time when it was hard to come out. He held on to that nugget for a long time, even though most of us knew.

Luis was a beautiful boy, and his mom, Cindy, was the prettiest mom I'd ever met. He was one of the wealthier kids in class, and his family traveled a lot. Although he wasn't American (shout-out to Danielle Oberdick, the only other American student in our grade!), his accent was perfect. He hung out with us little gringas more than anyone else, and I always got the feeling he felt more relaxed around us than the others.

In middle school, the three of us talked about sex. What we thought it was. Whenever one of us learned something new, we'd update the others. Luis always knew the most. I always knew the least.

Luis was funny and charismatic. Still, he struggled with depression his entire life and, as I recall, with feeling like he belonged.

Once, on a school field trip to El Morro in Old San Juan, Luis and I and another school friend were squeezed together on a small ledge, above one of the most treacherous, rocky areas of the Atlantic Ocean. Luis had looked so sad that whole day. I now believe he may have been having a depressive episode, but, at the time, *sad* was the only way it would have registered.

He'd been wearing a bucket hat, one he loved, when suddenly I saw it tumbling down to the ocean below. It *was* rather windy up there, but I thought I saw him throw it. I wasn't sure.

"Oh no! Luis! Your hat?"

"I wish it were me instead," he replied. He looked forlorn. I wish we would have reassured him, or asked why he said that, but I think we just sat there in silence. We really had so little concept of mental health struggles back then and behavior like this might have just been considered "dramatic."

Luis and I spent a lot of time in or by the water together, and we'd sometimes play a game called Frutita in our backyard pool with Danielle, my older sister, Zhena, and my parents. In Frutita, someone stood outside the pool with their back turned to everyone in the water and called out different fruits. If the fruit they called matched the one you secretly assigned yourself (banana!), you had to cross the pool as quietly as possible. But if they heard a splash? Chaos. They'd whirl around, and suddenly the pool would be a flurry of arms, legs, and panicked shrieks as everyone scrambled to make it to the wall before getting tagged by the fruit announcer. Whoever got caught became the next leader.

Just hearing the word *frutita* is enough to make me smile. It reminds me of simple, uncomplicated mirth—of the splashing water and the breathless squeals of kids living entirely in the moment. No angst, no heaviness. Those reprieves were sacred.

Luis and I tried to be sophisticated together, in the way that unsophisticated people are trying on a persona that doesn't quite fit. We sipped white grape juice like it was wine and uttered nonsense about things we didn't understand with the confidence of a presidential candidate offering campaign promises before an election. We may or may not have studied *Playboy*s together once, "for educational purposes." Luis was gay and I'm straight, so in retrospect I'm not sure whom this benefitted.

Luis ended up switching schools in tenth grade and I heard from him less frequently, but we'd still hug each other tightly whenever we saw each other. When we were sixteen, Luis came out to me by telling me about his first sexual encounter. He waited for me to update him on how far I'd gone sexually, which was absolutely nowhere. I was too embarrassed to tell him that, though, so I made up a story about a sloppy first kiss with a boy I'd met at camp. "So much tongue!" I said.

"Teenage boys!" Luis replied, mock-appalled. "Way too eager."

Now that Luis went to a different school and was sexually active, I wondered, was he too cool for me? Was this going to be the end of our friendship? I still thought of him fondly and still invited him over for Friday afternoon pool parties at my place. Yet somehow he seemed older than the rest of us. He fit in less and less, and eventually we drifted apart and he stopped coming.

When I went to college in Texas, my parents—still in Puerto Rico—would run into him at the local grocery store and send me updates about his life. Luis and I caught up on AIM from time to time.

NavainPR: Babe! Are you there?

LuigiChez: Babe! I miss you! How's college?

NavainPR: It's the greatest. Mostly because there's this hot guy in my French class who sounds just like Matthew McConaughey. I think I'm in love! How are juuuuu?

LuigiChez: Time for a BJ?

NavainPR: lol LUIS!

When we were nineteen years old, Luis died under tragic circumstances. That part of his story is not mine to tell.

What I can share is that Luis's death marked my first real encounter with sudden loss. In a way, it seems fitting that the person who was a friend when I needed one most would also be the one to help prepare me for the greatest loss of my life—the death of my mother.

I wasn't sure if I would write about Luis in this collection. I don't often tell people about him. I don't always know how to bring him up. But I want to change that. I want to talk about him more frequently. Honor him. Besides, how could I write a collection of essays about my tween/teen years and not include a tribute to my beautiful Luigi?

Luis Oscar Sanchez, I love you. I miss you.

Thank you for being my friend when I needed you most.

GRIEF

PENN

The first week we started recording for *Podcrushed* in the spring of 2021, we began with what was supposed to be the fun part. If you're a day one—that's a fan from day one, Mom—you'll remember that every episode of season 1 included a real story from one of our listeners, narrated by me (iconic king) with some punchy sound effects and music by our trusty engineer and music producer, David. We were still kicking this idea around, not sure how to best capture the middle school zeitgeist from the submissions we received, but the point was undoubtedly to Be Funny. There were a few stories with a sobering gravity we loved, but stories of grief weren't how we believed we should introduce ourselves. We thought our listeners would want to laugh.

Waiting for Nava, Sophie, and David to arrive for our first recording session on an overcast early spring day in Los Angeles, I sat at the head of a very long wooden table—archetypically long, *Game of Thrones* long. It was a halved tree trunk, nestled in the grotto-like succulent garden of a very strange and vibey house in

Venice I was renting with my wife and our two boys. A healthy distance from Hollywood, I was nonetheless filming the third season of *You* in the middle of the pandemic before the vaccines came. It was a surreal and intense period, being so isolated with a newborn and an eleven-year-old, especially while the stringency of COVID protocols for my work demanded that we be a very conservative COVID family. My wife and I would every so often host a friend or two at Aragorn's table in the garden, evidently made for socially distant dining if not plotting a siege. Underneath the table was a spider colony, so we didn't sit at this table any other time. Never. Our Siberian husky would often lie on it like a dead horse with his limbs sticking straight out, or perch sphinxlike and regal with his legs crossed (always evoking *Game of Thrones* imagery) but no human being felt natural or casual sitting at this grand, rotting, spider-infested outdoor table. Preparing to push this super-duper fun podcast of mine into existence, however, I found myself sitting down at the head with a transcendent gaze, uncharacteristically free from any fear of spiders.

I had just received news that struck me like lightning. The girl with whom I'd had my first real relationship—having dated for five of our teenage years, undoubtedly one of my closest friends from youth—had died at thirty-three, ultimately from the effects of twenty years of alcohol abuse. She had been my girlfriend, and I her boyfriend, and we'd spent our teens in Hollywood together as young actors. We'd parted ways at nineteen in the fall just before my birthday in November, and by August of the next year I'd moved to New York City to film *Gossip Girl*. I never returned to live in Los Angeles, so she and I knew almost nothing of each other as adults.

Throughout my twenties in New York, the fears I'd had about

her well-being subsided, and I often imagined her having recovered. I assured myself that her suffering, which I'd known so intimately in our youth, was surmountable. Evidently, it was not. Far from natural or inevitable, her death had explicit causes, and to ignore them would be to ignore her suffering as so many did when she was growing up. When we met, she was already struggling to accept the slow onset of failure in a career she had never chosen of her own volition, in a city whose value system could only make more empty promises to her and anyone she knew. The memories I have collected here are, in part, a recognition of her suffering, a testament to her resilience in the face of despair. She was denied a childhood, as well as a life into maturity, and so I choose to remember the youth she did have.

Her name was Keira. Unlike me, Keira had truly grown up in Hollywood, within less than a three-mile radius from where we met at fourteen in Burbank, California. I had just moved there with my mother into a beige-stucco apartment building after having spent our first year in a Los Angeles trailer park where, deeper in the Valley, we had been mercifully removed from Hollywood as a state of mind. In Burbank, however, we were embedded and unprepared. We lived in one of the many suburban nooks of what is otherwise the sprawling studio-industrial complex that serves as the massive and woefully afflicted heart of Hollywood, where Warner Brothers, Disney, Universal, ABC, NBC, and Nickelodeon, to name a few, all have their studio lots and where their executives lunch but never dinner. We had moved just down the street from the Warner Brothers lot, whose iconic water tower was visible from our first apartment. The Disney Channel high-rise was just as close, and huge, the most prominent feature on the horizon.

This was where I was nearly cast, time after time, in one ever-so-cheaply produced juggernaut tween series after another. I was wholly uninterested in pursuing such a career, but there wasn't a single actor I knew, young or old, who felt they had the agency to turn down an audition. I didn't, either. Shortly after booking my first lead in a television series on a now-defunct network called The WB, I would withdraw my own cash money for the first time from an ATM, and it was in the shadow of the Disney Channel high-rise. I pulled out two hundred dollars to buy, among other things, two ounces of weed. I probably smoked much of that weed with Keira.

Keira's mother was a very small woman and had been a stunt double for children before Keira was born. As soon as Keira could feasibly memorize a word of dialogue, she was ushered into show business. She booked her first role at age five and worked consistently in film and television until she was ten or eleven, landing roles in a few big films and working alongside actors and directors of the highest pedigree. By the time I met her, Keira would never work again like she had as a child. Her dreams of being an actor for the rest of her life were built on the reasonable expectation she could succeed because, in many ways, she already had. But the bizarre and unjust truth was emerging that her professional prime was behind her, and although this was no reflection of her creative or personal integrity, it must have felt like it to her. She was washed up by the time she hit puberty.

We met as any fourteen-year-olds do: by sheer circumstance. Our apartment complex, the Ashmoor Apartments, had something like 150 units in it, so it was a world unto itself for the twenty or so kids who lived there ranging from eight to fifteen years old—every one of us actors, and every one of us homeschooled. At the heart of this unstructured micro-community of professional minors, there were six boys aged thirteen or fourteen, myself included. We were the emergent brat pack of the Ashmoor. We roamed the place like no one else was interested in doing. Through no other social force than coincidence—or laziness—everyone we knew seemed to live on the west side of the complex. Keira moved in on the east side. Before this, our group rarely spent time on the east side, which had, improbably, a mysterious and unknown quality to it. Keira's appearance only underscored this impression.

Before knowing anything about her, Keira had, to me, the aura of a sweet girl from the wrong side of the tracks. My perception at fourteen could just as likely have been incorrect and paternalistic, but there happened to be a dimension of truth to it beyond her living on the other side of the complex. Keira had suffered already at fourteen the way relatively few people do. Furthermore, she was alluring to all the boys. She had striking blue eyes which always seemed to be looking up from her ever-so-slightly downturned face, framed by bleached-blond hair parted down the middle. Being 2001, this was an era of extremely low-waisted, very thin stretchy jeans, and baby-tee midriffs that left most of Keira's tanned, teenage torso exposed, her belly-button ring winking in the California sun. As a fellow teenager, I didn't object at all to her choice of attire.

Keira's arrival doubled the population of girls who were exactly our age. There was a gaggle of younger girls I remember fondly as children we didn't want to be around, and a few nineteen-year-old goddesses floating about the complex who were untouchable, but Keira was the New Girl. There is nothing else that catches the attention of fourteen-year-old boys more.

Every group has its pusher man. Ours was Mitchell. Mitchell

made sure we played Truth or Dare with Keira in the first few days of meeting her. He was a kind-hearted boy who, like all boys, carried various traits of masculinity that were still immature and unaware. Had we been any older, the way Mitchell badgered Keira until she relented and showed us her boobs would have felt more disconcerting. Some of us would have resisted, and Mitchell himself may have felt the sting of misogyny and entitlement in his persistent requests. Somehow, though, everyone we knew agreed it was part of his charm. Mitchell was a ladies' man. There was a simple and harmless name for what he wanted, anyway, what the whole group of boys came to expect: flashing. A harmless name for a harmless act. Not only, Mitchell insisted, was it a) totally normal, and b) not a big deal, but he had *dared* her. He was only following the letter of the law, and what could Keira do but oblige?

Keira and I started gravitating toward each other from the beginning, so we both entertained this common hazing process—Truth or Dare with the new girl to see who she would hook up with—because she and I wanted to hook up. Prompted by another dare, we had our first kiss within days in front of the other boys. When she finally flashed a few of us, I sensed we had reached a tipping point, and that her will was being tested in a way that didn't feel good. What was next? The game needed reining in. Keira and I took control of the situation the only way two extremely confrontation-avoidant fourteen-year-olds in 2001 understood how.

Once the rest of the boys found out Keira had flashed us, they naturally demanded for themselves equal opportunity. We knew this was coming. Keira and I couldn't speak about it explicitly, or even tacitly, but we both felt a dread. Operating by our adolescent logic and unaware of the precedent we were setting for ourselves, we knew she wouldn't have to do this anymore if she was mine (subtext of possession being, unfortunately, the point). So, with the few remaining boys configured in a row, Keira stood with me behind her, took my hands in hers, placed them on her bra, and together we exposed her breasts to the group for three seconds.

I don't know what boys, or even men, expect to gain in a moment like this. For us, there was only loss. For a few moments there was dull silence that, in my memory now, is overwhelming and oppressive. It was the sound of confusion for the boys: Is that it? For Keira and me, it was the sound of regret and apprehension; a small defeat we endured for what we thought would be a greater win.

It did turn out to be a relief for everyone, but not because the boys had finally seen an exposed nipple. After all, for an adolescent boy, seeing his first boob is the beginning of a relationship with a wound that will not heal; an appetite for boob is never actually sated by boob. Perhaps we remember a time when a nipple was our only sustenance, a true fount of life, an actual satisfaction of every need, and we wish to regain such a bountifully wholesome relationship with the female anatomy, or even our own mothers. Yes, perhaps. Whatever the case, this group of boys was relieved because Keira was clearly no longer an object for the group to pursue. She was with me. They could relax and finally become friends with her and behave somewhat like normal people. Now, rather than being ferally consumed by the possibility of seeing Keira's boobs at any given moment, they would only demand to be notified whenever I got to see them, or any other part of Keira's body.

Our closest friends would be, for years, far too concerned with what Keira and I were doing with our bodies—not only because all teenagers are like this, but because we were the first couple from the group to enter a long-term relationship. One such friend couldn't understand why we hadn't had sex yet (having never had sex himself), so one afternoon he demanded that Keira stick her hand down my pants when we were standing in an alley smoking cigarettes we'd found.

Just as Keira was pressured to bare her chest, this sent a dark feeling through me for reasons, again, I couldn't yet name or understand. I felt like I had to enjoy it—and that I should enjoy it—but I wasn't allowed the personal, social, or cultural space to wonder honestly why I didn't. Such a question was, in the early 2000s, synonymous with asking myself if I might be gay. The space for a boy becoming a man to explore his authentic desires for love and its manifold expressions are pitifully narrow—even still today, I believe. Young boys are highly sexualized, possibly as much as young girls are; it just hits different. Boys are expected to crave sex so indiscriminately that, although they're finally being taught about consent today, they often don't realize that they, too, can say No.

For all the sexual energy coursing on the surface between Keira and me, we were both quite patient, even timid, when it came to the pursuit of intercourse. Like so many things between us, we rarely spoke about sex directly. Neither of us felt it was possible to express clearly, or simply, what we wanted for ourselves and from each other. From the moment we met, we had shared a subconscious bond that did much of the communicating for us.

One night, in my bedroom, Keira was able to make it conscious. Under the Christmas lights I had strung up underneath my loft bed year-round, we lay clothed but entwined on the carpet, listening to a Yusef Lateef record. These were the sounds of a man communicating with the Divine through wordless acts, and taking his time. With her head tucked into my neck and her eyes closed, given permission by the softness of our conversation and the sweetness of our silence, Keira told me about the sexual abuse she had endured as a child.

I listened quietly. I could feel her tears flowing warm and free into a little pool around my clavicle and spilling over behind my neck, and the warm tickle of her breath so close to my skin as she whispered what she had been waiting to tell someone who could listen. I held her tightly as she described the man who had done this to her routinely.

He had been a family friend. The few adults in Keira's life had turned away from her when she'd tried to tell them. At nine years old, with no other recourse she could see, she stabbed her abuser in the leg with a knife. The whole family got the message, but Keira got very little response. The man abusing her disappeared, never reporting the incident or going to the hospital. His absence was barely recognized by her mother, nor was anything ever adequately addressed by the only other adult in Keira's life—a man named Jim who was not her mother's boyfriend or partner, but who was, evidently, a friend who helped take care of Keira. Jim died a year or two after the awful revelation of what had been happening to her.

I don't know anything about Jim other than that he was in the military and that he did take care of Keira in ways her mother, pitifully, could not. Keira spoke of Jim the way people speak about their fathers. She loved and missed him. That Jim was the most caring adult in Keira's life is a very bitter pill. The man who abused Keira was Jim's friend, so Jim was responsible for introducing him to the family. The guilt he and Keira's mother felt was terrible, and it is this guilt that compounded the family's collective trauma, setting the stage for the evolution of Keira's emotional abuse from her mother as she prepared to enter adolescence. It was for many years a marvel to me that a little girl could endure so much pain and that her mother—a miserable drunk—would find ways to treat Keira that felt, impossibly, more insidious than the sexual abuse she had suffered.

I can't ignore, change, or soften the fact that our relationship was seriously injured, before it ever began, by the effects of trauma. Our youth was made solemn by the impact of irresponsible adults and caretakers in our lives. I have tried to weave a different narrative, but the memories of our time together are all like this. In an attempt to show restraint, I have left out quite a lot—not only from Keira's narrative, but from my own. There were experiences I had as a child that enabled me to understand her trauma implicitly, though I did not have much conscious memory of mine at the time. I could only hold space, intuitively, for hers.

We belonged to a generation of young actors, many of whose life experiences and family systems didn't seem to be drastically different from ours (though Keira's was particularly extreme). My closest male friend, Everett—my best friend—also lived in the Ashmoor, and the three of us formed something of a trio. Our lives were threatened by the aimlessness and fear of failure that hangs like a heavy sword above any actor's head (the younger the actor, the heavier the sword). We didn't go to school. If we weren't working, what did we have to do? To self-soothe and generate excitement, everyone we knew turned to substances of one form or another. Keira drank enough that, at fourteen, she was hospitalized with alcohol poisoning for the first time. I smoked weed, and I'd started so early and smoked so much that by the time we were seventeen, I had to stop or risk what felt like an impending anxious-psychotic break.

Everett developed an opioid addiction on top of his alcoholism and, as our teenage years progressed, the television jobs he used to book regularly began to dry up. He would, in our midtwenties, attempt suicide. This was not a terrible surprise to me, but it was absolutely terrible.

Nearly a decade later, Keira's death did not surprise me, either. News like that shocks the nervous system, and there is grief, but there is no tortured bewilderment as to how or why this has happened. I was always pushing my fear for my friends' lives to the furthest corners of my mind. I realize now that if I feared this much for their lives then, I must have feared for my own. I may have survivor's guilt, or it may be an acute awareness of the perils we faced growing up together. Or I have a grudge. I have long held Hollywood and its value system in contempt, but since hatred doesn't help anyone or anything, I'm trying to let it go.

There is poignancy in my friends' resilience. At various stages of youth, through our success as working actors, all three of us had become financially independent and partly or wholly responsible for one or both of our parents. Keira and Everett were both five years old when they began acting professionally. That is exceptional, and by no standard a failure. I was twelve when I turned pro, and I wouldn't become financially independent until I was fifteen—practically geriatric in comparison—but I also started finding success at the same age they started experiencing their decline. Neither Everett nor Keira enjoyed gainful employment as actors past age twenty, although Everett would continue honing his craft, quite honorably, in classes and other experimental avenues. Keira, on the other hand, finally abandoned the chimeric pursuit altogether—a triumph in itself.

Keira and Everett had both started acting at an age that almost no one has ever carried on to lifelong success. They were exceptional children. Who was to say they were they not becoming exceptional adults? By what other than the most superficial metric had they failed?

There is one metric whose criteria feels cruel, given the preternatural ultimatum child actors face between school or work: a college degree. I don't know who among the Ashmoor's brat pack, or the wider Burbank network of young actors, ended up going to a university except Keira. With a little help from my mother and me, she forged a serious opportunity to get outside of the vicious cycle that ensnares so much of young Hollywood. I had started attending classes at Santa Monica College, a community college, just around the same time Keira and I met. If you recall from my previous essays, the process works like this: take the California High School Proficiency Exam (CHSPE), gain the equivalent of a high school diploma, attend community college, gain credits until you can transfer to a university, then apply to schools. Take as much time, or as little, as you want.

Although I was able to start this process much younger than most because of some tests from my short-lived middle school era, anybody could do this at sixteen (the only requirement for the CHSPE). I seemed to be the only young actor we knew at the time whose mother had connected these dots and who himself was interested in an alternative pathway to an already alternative pathway.

The drug of Hollywood is the belief that you will be among the exceedingly tiny minority who make it. Schooling is considered by many to be an obstacle, or an uninteresting detail, because this is a career that doesn't require any. As such, countless homeschool programs proliferated in Southern California at the turn of the millennium to meet the needs of scores of children caught in the frustrating tension between schooling and filming—neither could allow time for the other. These homeschooling programs were what all our friends in Burbank seemed to be enrolled in. I would venture to say that nearly every one of these programs was bullshit (sorry, not sorry).

Keira was very smart. Many young actors are. One needs, at least, significant emotional intelligence to be even a decent actor. So, at my and my mother's encouragement, and to Keira's mother's chagrin, she took the CHSPE when she turned sixteen, passed, and began attending classes at Santa Monica College, too. Some classes we attended together, creating a kind of high school sweetheart experience in community college. I was able to drive her to school—a full ninety minutes on most days, thanks to Los Angeles traffic—and our newfound independence was only an issue every third or fourth day when her mother decided I was kidnapping Keira and would threaten to call the police to report my license plate for an abduction. On one occasion, Keira's mother threw herself in the pathway of my car as I reversed out of the underground garage of our apartment complex, and I hesitated before braking.

Like I said, high school sweethearts.

Keira gathered the credits and applied to all the schools she could in nearly half the time I did—she'd started two years later—with UCLA and UC Berkeley as her top two, both with a psychology major. In the weeks we were hoping for her letters of acceptance, she got nothing. So much time passed that we could only assume she hadn't been accepted. This was dispiriting, to state the obvious, until one evening when acrid smoke filled her apartment, triggering the fire alarm, and Keira and her mother had to evacuate. What the firefighters discovered after their arrival (and much hubbub around the Ashmoor Apartments) was a stack of papers stuffed into the broiler: all of Keira's college acceptance letters. Her mother had attempted to hide that Keira had been accepted to both UCLA and UC Berkeley, and Berkeley had even offered her a full scholarship.

Both schools are great. But for some perspective here, UCLA was even closer to home than Santa Monica College. Of the nineteen different routes you might take to avoid traffic between the Valley and Santa Monica, at least three of them pass UCLA at about the halfway mark. The campus is a stone's throw from probably a dozen buildings where Keira and I had grown up going to auditions. UC Berkeley, on the other hand, is a nearly six-hour drive from Los Angeles without traffic, and it's not even in what you can call Southern California anymore. It's Northern California.

What Keira had achieved was incredible. She had defied the odds stacked against her, defied her mother's active resistance and, in the case of UC Berkeley, she had an opportunity to extricate herself—for free—from a home and an environment that was, in retrospect, mortally dangerous. From my thoroughly biased perspective, that was always the goal: find a way to get out of this town that has been your actual hell and start reorienting yourself in a tangibly different place, many hours away, surrounded by different people, engaging with a different value system from the one in Hollywood, and free yourself from your mother. Get. Out.

Citing her relationships with me and her mother, though, Keira decided to stay close to home and go to UCLA. To me, this was inconceivable. I felt like Keira had shut the door on herself, and my

Third grade graduation. Eight years old, spring of 1995. I look as though I just found out we're about to move over three thousand miles away.
PHOTOGRAPH BY LYNNE MURPHY

My mother says she took this shot moments after I found out I booked the role in *The Music Man*, summer of 1995. Apparently, I've been ambivalent about my work from the beginning.
PHOTOGRAPH BY LYNNE MURPHY

Fifth grade, teeth and hair both parted wide in the middle, late 1996.
COURTESY OF LYNNE MURPHY'S PERSONAL COLLECTION

My last year playing soccer, c. 1996. Zoom in on that group shot, I look absolutely perplexed. This boy had no plans for a life in front of the camera.
COURTESY OF LYNNE MURPHY'S PERSONAL COLLECTION

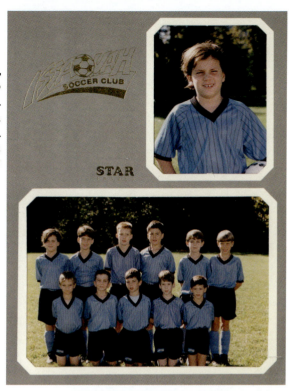

I'm sixteen here, and felt as serious as I looked, c. 2003.
PHOTOGRAPH BY LYNNE MURPHY

Riding horses with my siblings at a time and place where child safety regulations were not a concern. Pakistan, 1996.
PHOTOGRAPH BY DALE RUTSTEIN

Looking dapper with the whole family at a Holy Day celebration in Haifa, 1999. That's me on the left in the crop top with Dad, Siria, Mom, and Kalan.
COURTESY OF DALE RUTSTEIN'S PERSONAL COLLECTION

Walking under Siria's wing with Kalan (left) and Mom following closely behind, 2002.
PHOTOGRAPH BY DALE RUTSTEIN

Visiting Granddad (left) in London with Mom, c. 2003.
PHOTOGRAPH BY DALE RUTSTEIN

The last time I wore braids, on the beach with Siria (left), Mom, cousin Louisa, and Kalan, 2007.
PHOTOGRAPH BY DALE RUTSTEIN

Dad and I, 1984. In lieu of an entire essay he gets this photo. Love you, Dad!
COURTESY OF THE KAVELIN FAMILY'S PERSONAL COLLECTION

My parents, Farahnaz and Tommy, in their new home in Los Angeles, right before deciding to move to Puerto Rico, 1988.
COURTESY OF THE KAVELIN FAMILY'S PERSONAL COLLECTION

The last photo Zhena and I took together before moving to Puerto Rico. Los Angeles, 1988.
COURTESY OF THE KAVELIN FAMILY'S PERSONAL COLLECTION

One of the first family photos in our new island home of Puerto Rico (spot the pixie cuts on Zhena and I), c. 1988.
COURTESY OF THE KAVELIN FAMILY'S PERSONAL COLLECTION

My first Halloween with Zhena on the island, 1988—why the pixie cuts, dead mom?!
COURTESY OF THE KAVELIN FAMILY'S PERSONAL COLLECTION

Me and Mom in Spain for a weeklong holiday during the middle of the school year, c. 1990. Mom pulled me and Zhena out because she thought the life experience would be more valuable than the school lessons we were covering that week.
COURTESY OF THE KAVELIN FAMILY'S PERSONAL COLLECTION

In my living room during Ariana's first trip to Puerto Rico, c. 2000.
COURTESY OF THE KAVELIN FAMILY'S PERSONAL COLLECTION

own sensation of being entrenched began to overwhelm me. My desire to escape was only given satisfaction when I was working.

Being on a film or television production, ironically, is in some ways *not* like being in Hollywood—because you're working. Most people in Hollywood are not working on an actual Hollywood production. I never went long without a job of some kind, and by seventeen I was regularly leaving California for months at a time to shoot a show or a movie on location. Every time I left, I wanted to stay gone. I was being shown glimpses of another life—albeit one that was enabled by the belly of the beast—but I knew another life was possible. I wanted Keira to glimpse a vision of another life, too.

I'd long believed that new lives for both of us demanded that we end our relationship, but I had no idea how to make such a monumental shift and feared that I would be abandoning Keira in an uncaring wilderness. Or did I fear that I would be abandoned? For two years, I grappled with the weight of this decision, and I don't recall in that period speaking about it to anyone. Just like the suffocating threat of failure went conspicuously unspoken of in our young Hollywood circles, so did this. As an adult, I still marvel that there wasn't a single person with whom I felt I could unburden myself for even one heartfelt conversation regarding my relationship with Keira—namely, her. Why couldn't Keira and I address this together? What did we think our partnership was for if not for helping each other through something like *this*? This is the same period I stopped smoking weed, because, whenever I did smoke, I felt like I was going to buckle under the pressures I perceived in my life: of making money, of forging a worthwhile career, and managing the entanglement between Keira and me. I have never felt older than I did in these years.

When Keira moved into the dorms at UCLA, she at least gained distance from her mother. She also gained a roommate from Panama named Isla, who was bright and seemingly untroubled (and who offered Keira an unusually positive friendship). In the fall semester of her second year, however, Keira decided to move back in with her mother to save money. This was the beginning of the end.

We were nineteen, and I was enduring my longest period without work ever—nearly a year. In the previous two years, I had lived in Vancouver, then New York City for five months, respectively, while working on two short-lived television series (*The Mountain* followed by *The Bedford Diaries*), which provided me with a much-needed reprieve from Los Angeles. When I returned from New York City just after my eighteenth birthday, I found my own apartment in Van Nuys, thirty minutes away from our old stomping grounds in Burbank. To save money, I sacrificed things like cable and home internet and ate Taco Bell every day. I lived a spartan life that, after a year, I was starting to enjoy as it branched out into new adult friendships and began to naturally preclude my old patterns with Keira.

On an otherwise ordinary Wednesday night, I picked Keira up on campus in Brentwood after her class and drove her home to her mother's apartment where, in all our years together, I had never been allowed to spend longer than five or ten minutes. As I made a lefthand turn from the freeway exit ramp onto Pass Avenue, a turn I'd made thousands of times since I was thirteen years old—now only weeks away from my twentieth birthday—I broached the topic of our burdened relationship. A moment later I made a right-hand turn onto Heffron Drive, where Keira and I had lived as neighbors for the entirety of our teens. Continuing our conversation, I circled the block and finally parked my car around the corner from the entrance to the Ashmoor Apartments, where we had met for the first time. As I did this, I realized I'd never sat in a parked car on this particular block, one I'd walked endlessly throughout adolescence. It felt, somehow, different and very new. There, we finished the conversation, and with it, our nearly five years together.

We stayed in my car for a while, inside the tiny three-mile radius where Keira had lived fifteen of her nineteen years. It's a dense bubble straddling two micro-neighborhoods of Burbank on either side of the 134 Freeway: one called Toluca Lake and another that didn't have a name then but is now fittingly called Media City. At the center of this radius was a Vons supermarket whose massive parking lot was where we, and all the kids we knew, had countless firsts: alcohol, cigarettes, Starbucks, weed, porn, sex, and, as the French say, *et cetera*. The parking lot was winged on one side by an outlet strip where we could eat and loiter, and on the other was a bar called Marlo's and a Bank of America.

Marlo's had one darkened window and even to us—fourteen-year-olds who chugged Venti Frappuccinos and smoked cigarette butts we found on the street—it seemed like a thoroughly depressing and undesirable place to spend one's time. At some point in our early teens, a man walked out of Marlo's and into the parking lot of *et cetera* to fatally shoot himself in the head. Evidently, this lot of ours was not only an Eden of firsts, but of lasts.

I didn't get to know Keira into adulthood, a young woman who, many years later, ended up working as a hostess at Marlo's after it closed and reopened with a new name. I would love to find exquisite symmetry in such a development, a triumphant signal that Keira had remained where she was but transformed her reality regardless—that she could write a new script for herself, overcome her alcoholism, and discover a life of meaning free from the vise grip that the entertainment industry has always had in a place called Media City.

She may have. There may be those who only knew Keira in adulthood and choose to remember her as free in that way. It may be an awful shortcoming of mine that I am unable to. For me, there is her alcoholic death that horribly vindicates the fear I had for her life when we were kids. The eerie fact remains that, at thirty-three, she died the exact same way her mother had eight years earlier. Placed on an equal timeline, alcohol killed Keira long before it killed her mother, who was in her sixties when she died. That is a cycle of trauma *worsening*. I can't overlook that, and it is most definitely not what we were imagining for ourselves as we sat in my car and ended our relationship for the betterment of both our lives.

After our final moments together, I drove home in a daze before suddenly pulling into a church parking lot where I'd always admired a row of gorgeous trees, but where I had never, ever stopped. With my sunroof open, I stared up into the interlocking, kaleidoscopic fractal patterns of the leaves and limbs of a tree underneath an orange streetlight. Just as spontaneously as I'd pulled into this lot, I climbed up through my sunroof and scaled the tree where I found a nook to sit comfortably. There I stared into the night sky—always a sepia haze in the Valley—with the sunroof of my car open beneath me, Zero 7 softly playing from the speakers, and I saw the streets of my youth in a completely new light.

The night of Keira's death—the only time I've been able to connect enough to the grief to be able to shed tears—I closed my eyes, and what came to me was immediate, spontaneous, and very clear.

It was her. Not her image, but an experience of Keira's essence, an understanding. I perceived her character. She was so, so, so *light*. She was buoyant, and it was infectious. I laughed at how clearly I could see her. I had the simple and unshakable understanding that Keira had been like this all her life. The sly reveal here—because this essence visiting me also seemed to have a mischievous and quirky sense of humor—was that I had never known Keira very well. Neither had she known me, until this moment. So much of our personalities during our years together had been a coping mechanism in response to our environment, and the shortcomings of our childhood homes. This must be true for all adolescents to varying degrees, and for us it had simply been extreme.

If those who knew Keira in adulthood had just been saddled with a grief that would take years to process, I felt as though my grief had, after two decades, finally resolved—if only for a moment. I knew she was finished with it, too.

Through tears, I smiled and thought, *It's nice to finally meet you.*

I LOVE LOVE

SOPHIE

I've been on a mission to find "the one" for as long as I can remember. If I think back on my relatively short life, the whole thing seems to be covered in a rosy filter and littered with cartoon hearts. I blame at least a little bit of my obsession on my parents, married for thirty-nine years and still so in love with each other that they put most newlyweds to shame. I grew up hearing laughter and whispers from their pillow talk most nights, and if you ask my mom in earnest about their decades-long marriage, she *will* tear up. It's because of them that I *love* love.

Being international development workers, my parents carted me and my siblings across the globe. My childhood is marked as much by foreign languages, long-haul flights, and open-air markets as it is by at least one great love in each of the countries we lived in. The Confucius temple in Beijing and the islands of the Philippines were backdrops to some of my greatest heart *swells* and most epic heart *breaks*.

From an early age I was orchestrating romance between myself and various boys. When I was six, I forced a less than compliant friend in Haifa to hold a rose between his teeth as I led him in the tango one evening. We performed for our parents in the living room, who thought it was hysterical. There was nothing funny about it to me.

At age seven in Albania I chronicled the (imaginary) love triangle between myself, my elder sister's classmate, and the boy who sat across from me in school—a triangle I knew would have been fraught with homemade Valentine's Day cards and furtive glances across the schoolyard. When my sister and her friend secretly read my diary entries, they wrote a note back to me explaining that I was delusional. Their classmate had no clue who I even was. I read it and scoffed. *They* were delusional.

I had a dramatic relationship with a boy in the Philippines spanning years of both elementary and middle school. We hardly exchanged more than a surreptitious wave and a coy "hello" in the hallway, but I swore we were meant to be. Our tentative relationship came to a screeching halt when he confessed that he was gay and apologized for the fact that I was (of course) the last of my classmates to find out. And as you may already know, I managed to squeeze in a brief fling with Max Becker (certified hottie) just before leaving the country.

In my Beijing high school, I found what my mom referred to as "puppy love" with a strapping Swedish lad whose parents were also expatriates. When I was a junior, I was sure that this blond, blue-eyed, star-of-the-rugby-team senior in high school would eventually be my husband. I didn't care how many people brushed our relationship off as young love; I didn't even care that he himself was hesitant to ever respond *too* directly to my plans for marriage after college. I felt confident that I would be baking Swedish cinnamon rolls with his family every winter in Stockholm. Suffice to say, the only Swedish treats in my life today are the ginger cookies from the IKEA in Glendale, California.

This pattern continued into my twenties, much to my loved ones' concern. I looked everywhere for love, and when it came knocking, I almost always answered. The problem with welcoming love into your home is that, more often than not, it eventually gets up to leave again. In the best-case scenario, love slowly puts its shoes back on at the door and politely says goodbye, leaving as quietly as it arrived. But sometimes love blasts through your home like a tornado, turning over couch cushions and tracking the muddy wheels of its baggage over the hardwood floors of your life, and you find yourself on your hands and knees desperately trying to clean up the mess it has made.

The last time my heart was broken—I mean *really* broken, to the point where I felt it had been ripped right from my chest—I was twenty-two, going on twenty-three. For the second time in my life, I had fallen in love with a man nearly eight years older than me, whom we'll call Matt. That's right, at twenty-two I was on my *second* relationship with an older man. Dear reader, let me offer you some friendly advice . . . don't fall in love with a man eight years your senior when your frontal lobe hasn't finished developing.

I fell hard for Matt. He knew my older siblings, and we first met, very briefly, when I was just fourteen. But we had no contact again until the summer after my freshman year in college, when an email from him popped up in my inbox. A mutual friend had just visited me in New York and the visit had come up in their conversation with Matt, prompting him to write to me. The note ended with, "P.S. I found this email on Facebook so I hope it reaches you!" Matt and I started casually writing back and forth. A paragraph here and there turned into pages of text, although he would often take much longer than me to reply. I tried to hold off on responding, to match his detachment, but I always caved.

He was intelligent in a way that made me want to read, funny in a way that made me want to loosen up, and aloof in a way that made me want to cling to him. In the winter of my sophomore year, after many months of emails, Matt made an excuse to pass through New York so we could spend time together in person. I was absolutely charmed by him. On the final night of his trip, when my roommates had retired to their beds, we sat on my couch, just the two of us. Matt was the picture of calm, and I was a bundle of nerves. Either he didn't notice or he didn't mind my energy, because he looked me in the eye and said, "I want to spend more time together." Well, that was that. Matt and I started dating. A few months in, my parents could feel that the relationship wasn't quite right. They saw that I had an admiration and affection for him that wasn't matched.

They also saw that I was young, merely a college student, and I had many years ahead of me to meet someone who was a better fit. I agreed with my parents, but I already loved Matt, so instead of breaking things off, I confronted him about it. I asked why he seemed so guarded when my heart was so open. I told him, "I thought you were effusive . . . was I wrong?" He assured me that I wasn't, he really was a very emotional and sensitive person, but he had some things going on that prevented him from showing that to me. He was vague about what was causing this blockage, but I would soon learn it was serious enough to call everything into question, and very much validate my parents' concern. Unfortunately, by the time I found out, I was already hooked on him.

I remember stepping out of class one evening and receiving a call from my dad. He knew I was head over heels for Matt, but he tried to give me some perspective. "You're so young. You have years ahead of you to meet the right person. Everyone has got their own baggage. But when you marry someone, you take on their baggage, too. It clangs around in the trunk of your car for the rest of your life, so you want to make sure you know what you're signing up for."

He and my mom wanted to protect me from making the wrong decision, and when they realized I wasn't going to end it myself, they gave me their official stance: "We are *never* going to approve." Some daughters would have protested their parents' disapproval, and although I did not go down without a fight, I knew that, at the end of the day, continuing a relationship without my parents' consent was not an option for me.

On my way home from visiting Matt in the early months of 2016, it became clear the relationship would have to end. I spoke to my parents on FaceTime while I waited at my gate for the flight home, and they told me, once and for all, they would never give their consent. After landing, I called Matt on the train home from the Newark airport to officially end the relationship.

In the following weeks I processed my heartbreak out loud. I remember walking down a tree-lined block in Brooklyn and calling my father in tears. When you inhabit small spaces with roommates in every livable corner, your private life sometimes spills out into the streets. In a city of eight million people, no one is thinking twice about the girl crying audibly on the street. I made full use of the anonymity that living in New York affords you. I treated the city as an extension of my bedroom.

My father's advice to me on that teary call was the same as it had always been—to forget completely about the love of a partner. "You won't find love as long as you are clinging this tightly to it, my dear," he told me between my sobs. I had wrestled with this piece of advice for as long as my dad had insisted it was the surest way to find love. It's simply counterintuitive, and my mode of operation has always been to lead with emotion first and call on logic second. Besides, I *had* found love—many times, in fact. What I didn't realize at the time was that my obsession with relationships had kept me trying to work on even the ones that were doomed to fail.

Coming home from that trip to see my now-ex, I was a bleary-eyed mess. I had lost all concept of self-awareness or shame in the midst of my heartbreak. I didn't care who saw me in my lowest state; I didn't care about much at all. But as I walked in the door late that night, there stood David. A longtime friend of my roommate, David was staying at our apartment while on tour in the US with his band, Vallis Alps. Although he'd grown up in Washington State, David was currently living in Sydney, Australia. He and his bandmate had released their debut EP on SoundCloud one random Tuesday in 2015, and it had gone viral. They'd gotten significant radio support in Australia, so he'd followed the music.

He reminded me of a puppy dog—boundless energy and positivity, kind brown eyes and hair to match. David was good, and he was sweet, but I was nursing a broken heart and puffy eyes so, for perhaps the first time in my life, I saw none of that. After some obligatory small talk in the living room, I made a beeline for my bedroom, locked the door behind me, and wept.

The next night after finishing my seven p.m. class, Teaching Elementary Math, I walked twenty minutes from NYU to the Mercury Lounge on Houston Street where David's band was playing their show. David had texted me earlier that day to let me know I was "on the list," and I felt *very* cool relaying that to the bouncer at the door.

David surprised me with his stage presence. He had an easy confidence about him that I registered and logged.

After the show, a group of us made our way back to the apartment. We stayed up late, telling stories and munching on the strawberries David's manager had gotten from Trader Joe's earlier that day. David was particularly animated as he told us the story of a botched private show in Jamaica.

He and his bandmate, Parissa, had been hired to perform at an opulent wedding in a mansion on the beach. David had rented a velvet tux and bow tie for the occasion because he didn't have anything fancy enough in his own closet, but the moment they took the stage, a torrential downpour began (hardly a surprise for December in the tropics), and they never got to play a note.

He told the story standing up, while the rest of us stayed seated—more room for gesturing, I guess? I enjoyed watching him recount the details, even though I zoned out here and there as I noticed for the first time how cute he was.

As I sat there popping strawberries into my mouth, I felt an itch. It started on my arm, then moved to my leg, then my forehead. I sneaked off to my room to investigate in private. When I looked in the mirror, I saw that I was breaking out into hideous hives all over my face and body. I've since learned that I developed a late-onset allergy to strawberries in my early adulthood—and this was the moment it hit. I never emerged from my bedroom that night.

David left on a flight back to Australia early the next morning, and between the hives and tears, it felt as if we were circling each other without ever making a connection. But as all good millennials do after meeting, we soon added each other on every form of social media available to us. Including Snapchat.

Over the coming year, Snapchat would be the vehicle for a best-friendship to blossom between us. It began with quips back and forth in response to ten-second videos, and it grew into constant communication. Snapchat provided the balance of an intimate and honest look into each other's lives and senses of humor while also allowing us to keep things lighthearted. It was perfect—no romance, just funny, disappearing texts and videos. I put up no pretenses with Snapchat. Why bother? All of it vanishes without a trace.

Snapchat is, dare I say it, the most honest form of online communication. Of all apps, the Snapchat of 2016 mimicked a face-to-face conversation most accurately. When talking to someone in person, no one is recording what you say; there is no searchable document that logs your every word. The sentences and thoughts you share leave your lips and linger in the air for a moment before they are rearranged and interpreted by the other. Even if one recounts an in-person conversation after the fact, it's mostly the intangible feelings they are left with that are recorded. Exact words disappear, just like on Snapchat.

I was comfortable with my friendship with David developing over

Snapchat—it felt like I could keep him at a comfortable distance while I figured out what I wanted. With a few failed relationships under my belt, I had decided I needed to break my pattern. Previously, I had jumped headfirst into relationships, getting to know my partners *while* we were falling in love, so that by the time I saw any red flags, I was already attached and willing to look past them. When David and I began to write to each other, I could tell that there was chemistry, but my father's words were starting to get through to me, and I wanted to experiment with being friends first. Then Snapchat introduced Bitmojis.

All of a sudden avatars that David and I had each separately made in our own image could interact, even when David and I couldn't. We were oceans apart, yet we could ride horses side by side without ever getting up from the couch; we had only ever met in person once, during his brief stay at my apartment, yet our digital selves could stare into each other's eyes with just one tap. I was always *extra* careful not to accidentally use any of the lovey-dovey Bitmojis, but I certainly scrolled through them for myself. It was strange to see David and me (or our digital counterparts) interacting so intimately. I would be lying in bed in Brooklyn looking at Bitmojis of David and me blowing kisses to each other, and wondering if he ever scrolled through them like I did. Thousands of miles apart, I felt like David and I shared an intimate history.

We continued chatting constantly over Snapchat for the next eight months, never actually speaking about the obvious connection that was building. My mom was the first to notice the connection between David and me. When I was home for the holidays, she found me on the couch tapping away at my screen and asked,

"Who is it that's making you smile at your phone like that?" I was caught off guard.

"Oh, it's just David," I said. My mom made eyes at me, and I knew what she was wondering. "No, he's just a friend. He's like *so* just a friend I can't even describe it to you."

"Anyone who makes you laugh and smile like that is worth considering." She shrugged and left the room.

That comment stirred something in me. Why had I brushed David off as just a friend? Talking to him was easy and comforting, which I might have mistaken for "comfortable." At the time, I really didn't believe that deep love could spring from a friendship so lovely and nice. "Lovely," "nice," "easy," and "comfortable" are not the words used in literature to describe great loves. I was on the hunt for *passion*, *romance*, and *drama*. It wasn't only media that was steering me wrong; I had also been conditioned by a couple major relationships of my own to think that love needed to be tumultuous and dramatic to be meaningful.

While I was putting in the effort to convince myself that David was still just a friend, he let me know that Vallis Alps was coming back for another US tour in February, only a year after we'd last seen each other. My heart fluttered. We made sure to carve out some time to hang, just the two of us. Without addressing it yet, we both knew what was about to go down.

My roommates and I were at a Bahá'í gathering in Maine for the weekend when David, his bandmate Parissa, and manager Melody were arriving in Brooklyn. After some deliberation, I decided to leave the gathering a day early and hitch a ride back home with some friends attending the same meeting. My roommates stayed behind to finish out the rest of the sessions. Looking back, the decision to leave the gathering early was an important step in my and David's relationship—it was a commitment to see where things might lead.

The drive home from Maine was long, but when we started crossing familiar streets, I knew we were closing in on my neighborhood. Nerves crept in. David, Parissa, and Melody were staying at our place for the night, so arriving home meant seeing David in person again for the first time in a year. I texted to let him know I was close. David casually mentioned that Parissa and Melody were exhausted and had retired to their room for the night, implying that we would be alone. *Oh God.* I suddenly remembered I was a physical being with a body and a face that would soon be perceived. I hadn't looked in a mirror for over eight hours, but I just knew my hair had to be messy and my eyeliner smudged.

I zoned out of the conversation in the car and texted my roommate group chat. *Guys. I'm stressed!!* They responded immediately, keeping me company in the last few minutes of the car ride.

> **Jaspar:** How close?!
> **Taraneh:** Oh my god
> **Sophie:** 8 mins
> **Sophie:** I need to poop guys
> **Jaspar:** 😄😄😄😄
> **Taraneh:** Stress poop is the worst
> **Taraneh:** Squeeze your cheeks!
> **Sophie:** GUYS
> **Sophie:** I'm on Lafayette and Nostrand
> **Jaspar:** Yayyy
> **Taraneh:** Try to be in the moment! Love you!
> **Sophie:** Love you :')

At eleven fifteen p.m. I went dark on the group chat. We had arrived at my building, 126 Jefferson Avenue. I stepped out of the car with my things, said goodbye to my ride, and took a moment at the bottom of the stoop to collect myself. I peeked up to see my living room window dimly lit. *Here we go.*

I opened the door to the apartment and David was standing right there, ready to greet me. He must have heard my keys jangling. *No time for a mirror check.* My cramped New York City entryway meant that our bodies were already close. I fumbled with my bags and we hesitantly embraced. I was so bashful, I could barely look him in the eye.

We were both nervous to start, but it didn't take long for the air between us to thaw. Within fifteen minutes we had settled into a comfortable familiarity. We stayed up until two in the morning, talking and teasing each other. What stands out about that night (for both of us) is the nonstop grinning. Whenever there was a moment of quiet, one and then both of us would break into a smile. The grinning spoke volumes. Although we hadn't acknowledged it out loud yet, there was an undeniable connection between us, and we couldn't help but giggle over it. He and I both knew exactly what the grinning meant; it's the closest I've come to reading someone's mind.

We spent every spare moment together while he was in New York, both of us giddy and nervous in equal measure. The morning after I arrived home, we went for breakfast together at Emeline's, a diner that has since closed down. Over eggs and bacon, we talked about our families and our plans for the future, making sure to note that nothing was "set in stone," and we're "flexible should anything change." There were no horses or unicorns, no bubble letters spelling out "I LOVE YOU," no sparkly hearts popping up in my eyes as I looked across the table at his sweet face. It turns out life without Bitmojis is a lot less flashy.

The next day, after bounding around the West Village together, we sat down to rest in the NYU Bobst Library off Washington Square Park. It was the first moment of quiet in a day full of buzzing. We sat in swivel chairs across from each other in one of the many lounge areas of the library.

David looked me straight in the eye and said, "So, should we talk about it?" We both knew exactly what he meant.

I shrank into my chair. "Probably," I eked out. I didn't know if I was ready to have this conversation yet, but it was time.

"I'll go first," he started.

Whatever hesitation I had melted away as he spoke. I remember a distinct feeling of calm settling over me. It was almost like the air got thick and drifted down onto my shoulders. Not like a weight—more like a security blanket. It felt intuitive, and simple, and safe. It seemed in that moment like it had been written, our being together.

As much as I had resisted it previously, what led me to my greatest love was a focus on friendship. I have to say thank you to my mom, for opening my heart to David. And thank you to my dad, for encouraging me to loosen my grip on my idea of love so that it could come and find me, whole and happy.

Younger Sophie loved the thrill of a good flirt. She loved not knowing where something might go and the electric feeling before the first touch. She loved wondering who her person would be and sweeping, romantic declarations. My marriage has shown me that just as much meaning could (and would) come from a quieter joy and certainty. I love the steadiness of a consistent partner; I love connecting over a morning coffee, and I love watching a movie in silence. I love building on jokes so dumb no one else would understand and crying over how cute our baby is. I love keeping each other in check and saying, "I'm sorry," because I know I'll hear it, too. I love watching our daughter become David, and me, and someone else entirely. I love love.

THE IMAGINATIONSHIP

NAVA

In 1995, my friends Miguel, Kay, and Charity are involved in the *wildest* love triangle, and I've only recently been able to understand how much it has impacted me.

It's hard to even know where to start with these three. Miguel is this sweet, gorgeous, down-to-earth guy who's best friends with Kay. Kay is beautiful, brunette, and just realizing she might be in love with Miguel. She *wants* to tell him, but she's scared to. I relate to her predicament intensely because I'm in the same spot with Diego. I'm watching Kay for cues. Recently the vibes between Kay and Miguel are flirty, and I'm convinced they're days away from a full make-out sesh. Maybe even *one true love* status.

Enter Charity. Kay's cute blond cousin who moves to town. When Miguel meets her through Kay, he is *instantly* smitten.

If I'm being honest, Charity *is* really sweet, but I can't root for her. Number 1: Kay loved him first. Number 2: Charity is a blonde. (In the nineties, blondes are at the very top of the beauty totem pole, and as a rule, I can't root for the people already on top!)

Kay's feelings blossom into full-on obsession. I'm starting to feel a little nervous about her intensity, but I'm still rooting for her. (If Kay gets Miguel, doesn't that swing the whole universe in the direction of Nava-landing-Diego?)

As Charity and Miguel grow closer, Kay goes full soap-opera villain on them, trying everything she can to break Charity and Miguel up—curses, possession, setting literal fires. It's unhinged. Once Kay tricks Miguel into impregnating her (it's a long story), I fully tap out, and I'm still not sure how it all ended.

By the way, when I referred to this trio as my "friends" earlier, I probably should have said "the teenage stars of the short-lived NBC soap opera, *Passions*, with whom I had a parasocial relationship." But I did mean it when I said I've only recently begun to understand how this impacted me.

Passions was the first of a series of teen dramas (plus *Friends*!) I watched when I started to really latch onto the idea that even if someone you liked didn't see it at first, it was okay to hold on to those feelings. In most of the shows, the other party would come around for an epic first kiss and eventual love story. (See: *Dawson's Creek*, *Felicity*, *The O.C.*)

This imprinted the idea on me that true love could very well blossom from unrequited feelings. If someone was all-in too quickly, I would immediately tap out. I was distrustful of them. In fact, up until my thirties, if a guy liked me right away, I would get physically nauseous. I guess some part of me was pretty scared of a real relationship. It was much safer to play the lead in my imaginationships.*

For most of my life, imaginationships have been my preferred kind of relationship. I'm as well-versed at engaging in situations where I imagine things to be further along than they are as I am in projecting all of my hopes, fantasies, and idealized dreams onto a man who, in hindsight, is never that special.

If I had to pinpoint the origin of my proclivity for imaginationships beyond *Passions*, I'd probably start with my middle school years, when it felt like everyone around me was pairing up. My friends were starting to date—awkward but earnest hand-holding at lunchtime, make-out sessions after school—and I wasn't allowed to join in. My parents thought teenage dating was "pointless," and it was simply off the table. Instead of dating, I turned to teen dramas. Teenage romance, with its clichés and conveniently timed declarations of love, began to fuel my imagination, and by sixteen I couldn't imagine a greater moment in my life than the first time I would exchange *I love you*s with a teenage heartthrob and become his girlfriend.

That early mix of longing and fantasy didn't disappear as I got older—it only evolved, becoming a quiet undercurrent in my

---

* **imaginationship** *(noun)*
im·ag·i·na·tion·ship | \ i-ˌma-jə-ˈnā-shən-ˌship
   1. **Primary Definition:** A situation in which one person imagines the relationship to be more romantically significant, committed, or involved than it actually is.
   2. **Secondary Definition:** A relationship where one person projects their dreams, fantasies, and idealized version onto another, without fully engaging with the actual individual and their shortcomings.

relationships. The key ingredient to sustaining an imaginationship was avoidance. No matter how fiercely I liked someone, no matter how far along we were in spending time together, I could never bring myself to candidly express my hopes and desires or gain clarity on theirs.

In my thirties, after a series of painful, unrequited emotional entanglements and a series of wonderful men I rejected for banal reasons, I knew I had a problem. Even when I thought I had "done the work" (going to therapy, attending seminars on relationships, reading countless books, crying, praying, journaling) I learned I was still susceptible to wasting valuable time in an imaginationship.

After ending a relationship with a man who made bold proclamations of love but lacked follow-through, I thought I'd finally done it. I'd finally broken the pattern.

Then I met Parker.

• • •

Parker Finlay and I met over croissants through a mutual friend. I had come straight from working out—my cheeks were flushed, my hair a little frizzy, and my clothes oversized. Parker didn't ask for my number, and I forgot all about him. A month later, wearing makeup and clothes that actually fit, I bumped into Parker at an improv show. We ended up sitting together, and I felt an unexpected stirring in my chest when he leaned over to ask me a question. After the show, he followed me out of the building and lingered while I made lunch plans with my friend Lexi, who also happened to be at the show.

He chimed in, "I love Thai food," when Lexi and I decided to grab Thai. I tried not to chuckle.

"Wanna join us?" I invited him.

A month later, Parker and I were out to dinner alone for the first time. Things were going incredibly well until I asked him why he and his ex-girlfriend, Jessie Green, broke up. His eyes welled with tears.

Oh shit.

"I don't know." His entire demeanor shifted.

He went on to share a devastating story about an abrupt ending and a breakup that had shattered his heart along with all of his conceptions of love.

"I'm friends with all my exes except Jessie," he continued. "I unfollowed and blocked her on everything. I can't resist her pull when I'm in her orbit." He casually added, "I don't know if I'm ever going to love that way again. I guess now I'm just looking for a deep connection. She's the only woman I ever wanted to marry or have children with. I don't even think I want those things. I only wanted them with her."

His voice cracked with emotion as he uttered those last two words. He shifted in his chair, stopped making eye contact, and added very drily: "I've been dating all these multiple women, and I've been letting them all know I'm not looking for a relationship."

Was this not a date? Was he lumping me in with the multiple women? *All* these multiple women?

He added, "But I think I'm whittling it down to one."

If a guy had ever referred to me as the woman he'd whittled it down to, I would have castrated him. (Or sent my friends taunting memes about him.)

I should have asked him why we were even out that night, but me and avoidance were practically married at this point.

Well, this is over.

There was just one thing. One detail tripping me up.

Twenty minutes before basically admitting he was hung up on his ex, never going to fall in love again, and starting a harem, we were mid-conversation, debating something political. He was speaking, and he interrupted himself. He looked me dead in the eyes and said, "I want to do this many, many more times."

My heart rushed. *I wanted to do this many, many more times, too.*

"If you're not looking for a relationship, why are you 'whittling it down to one'?" I was trying to understand exactly how much of a red flag/potential friend he was.

"I dunno. 'Cuz you have to pick at some point, I guess. I can already foresee challenges in our communication style, but . . ." He shrugged. "What about you? What are you looking for?"

I looked at him defiantly. "I want to get married and have kids."

"Really?" he replied.

"Oh yeah!" I was filled with energy. "I'm ready. I feel like this is my season. Let's goooo!"

He laughed at my enthusiasm.

As we walked out of the restaurant together, I was sure we were never going to see each other again.

I felt sad.

We texted a little bit that night and the next morning, made tentative plans to see each other again, but a few days later I decided to let things go. If he followed up when he got back from a short trip, I was going to say no. I had been down the path with a man who wasn't ready multiple times before, and it always ended in heartbreak.

But when Parker got back and followed up, I decided there

was no harm in fostering a friendship. (*Remember, the key to an imaginationship is lying to yourself!*) We visited the Silver Lake Reservoir together. We laid down a towel and sat next to each other, but Parker wouldn't look at me. He was sitting as far away from me as he reasonably could.

"I've decided I'm not going to enter into any relationships because I'm moving to New York." He then shared about his love of the city and how alive he felt when he was there. He concluded by saying, "There is nothing and no one for me in LA."

He was wearing a sleeveless shirt that day. I was really into arms. His were really nice. I decided not to take his comments personally.

"New York is awesome! I loved living there. I've actually moved pretty often in my adult life, and I think it's great to gain new life experience. You seem pretty clear on what you want." I stopped short of offering to help him pack.

He shifted his body to face me and looked at me directly.

"Enough about me. How are you?" He smiled.

Oh. I definitely feel something.

When we went out a third time, I knew I was in trouble.

• • •

Parker left town for a five-week trip to New York. For the first three weeks, I felt uncharacteristically calm. We had time to figure this out. Even if he moved to New York, it wasn't the end of the world. A month into his trip, I was out to lunch with my cousin. I glanced down at my phone, and Parker had shared a memory of a game he used to play as a kid. Something about the story made my heart ache. He was a good man. I sneaked off to the restroom, stood in front of the mirror, and placed a palm to my chest. My heartbeat grew wild. *What was happening?*

Over the next few weeks, as my feelings escalated, panic crept in. I began wondering about the other women Parker was dating. Were they prettier than me? Was he sleeping with any of them? Was there someone in New York?

The fear eventually overtook me, and on July 14, at 6:33 a.m., exactly one day before Parker was coming back to LA—one day before we were set to spend the summer together going dancing, trying out LA's hottest bagel spots, and watching a series of movies we'd curated for each other—I brought things to an abrupt close. I texted him: I'm feeling discouraged, and I don't think we should hang out anymore... The reason I offered was that he hadn't replied to a message I'd sent offering to pick him up from the airport.

The *real* reason was that thirty minutes earlier, at 6:03 a.m., I logged onto Instagram to look up Taylor Tomlinson's account. She was our *Podcrushed* guest for the day, and I was curious to see if we could use a recent joke for a promo video. On the Explore page, about to type in Taylor's name, I noticed a little cartoon drawing on the top right of the screen. I clicked on it absentmindedly.

The cartoon was cute, clever. The account belonged to Jessie Green. We had one mutual friend—*Parker Finlay.*

At some point over those past six weeks, while we were getting closer and I was opening my inner world to him, Parker had refollowed Jessie and willingly floated back into her orbit.

My heart started pounding, and I was mad.
This is going to end in disaster.
I started typing a message. A tiny part of my brain said, *Hey,*

girl, he'll be back in town tomorrow. Take a beat and ask him about it then. I muzzled it.

I tried to incorporate the Jessie thing—the thing that was actually the thing—but I couldn't imagine a scenario where he wouldn't assume I was internet-stalking his ex. I typed up the airport thing. My heart beat furiously.

Are you sure you want to do this?

I wasn't.

Send.

Message failed to deliver.

What? I tried again.

Message failed to deliver.

Relief washed over me.

Oh shit! I don't want him to see these messages.

Undo send. Nothing happened. *UNDO SEND.* Nothing happened. I rushed to place my phone and laptop on airplane mode. I needed time to come up with a plan.

Maybe, I thought for a brief moment, I would just never take these off airplane mode.

Could I throw my devices into the Pacific and buy new ones? Move to a mobile-less land and learn the local ways, all to avoid these texts penetrating the ether?

Perhaps.

I tried very hard to ignore the reality that at some point those messages were going to reach him, but the panic attack still found me. I turned on the shower and let the hot water wash over me, opening up my lungs. I repeated a soothing prayer over and over again as I struggled to regain control over my breathing. An hour later, I was forced to turn my phone back on for work.

As soon as my internet connected, Parker Finley Parker Finley Parker Finley lit up my screen. I had forgotten about my Apple Watch, charging quietly in the corner. Sending out my destructive little messages.

Son of a bitch.

Hey, I have to admit it's pretty strange to get these messages from you. I don't want you to do anything that makes you uncomfortable but I'm a little confused . . . he began.

The term "strange" really pierced me.

Parker was right, and I needed to acknowledge it. I sent him a message owning up to my fear of getting hurt if we weren't on the same page. No mention of Jessie.

Three dots formed.

I held my breath.

I don't want anyone to get hurt. He wasn't fighting for us. He was letting it go.

I apologized for being strange and agreed to time apart. I told him I was feeling okay about everything and eventually I thought we could be friends again.

I cried all night.

· · ·

A month later, I reached out to Parker. He might be moving to New York, as he'd promised, and I wanted to see him before he went. I also invited him to join a media group that I thought he would enjoy. He was down for the group as long as I knew that the only thing he would ever want to pursue with me was friendship. He didn't want anything to get "blurry." His message hurt my feelings, but it lent me new determination to let go of the past and to focus instead on the future.

In October, I attended a weeklong seminar on overcoming anxiety in relationships. I got back to online dating and tried earnestly to form connections. I said yes to nearly every social invitation. Parker and I reconnected at a filmmaking space and briefly started texting again. But after the texts led nowhere, I realized he was just a distraction, and I decided it was time to delete his number and sever our connection. If my mind started to wander in his direction, I told myself *no* and shifted my focus to something different.

I went on daily walks and meditated along the path. I increased my efforts to serve my local community and ended up meeting two of my closest friends in the process. I engaged in a much more robust daily prayer practice, and for the first time that I could remember, I didn't feel anxious about my love life.

I could honestly say I was happy.

• • •

On the last day of November, I woke up to a text from an unknown number. Hey, it's been too long, it began. If you're up for it, maybe we can grab a coffee.

I assumed it was Darryl, the cute guy I had met the week before who'd grabbed my number and said he'd ask me out soon.

But why would he say "it's been too long"?

Must be a scam. *Screw those phone-scamming bottom feeders.* My finger hovered over block—a thought.

What if it's Parker?

Very gently, I lifted my finger off the screen.

I searched the media professionals' group chat that Parker and I were both a part of in my text messages. There was only one unknown number in the mix.

The numbers matched.

Excitement. Anger.

Well, I'm sorry, Parker. You can't just dart in and out of my life whenever you feel like it.

Thanks, but I'm not interested in scraps of your time and attention meted out as convenient for y— Erase, erase.

Too harsh.

It's been too long! How are you? I'm doing— Backspace, backspace.

Too friendly.

Sure, I'm up for a coffee catch-up. :) A deep breath.

Send.

We met up the very next day. He offered to pay, but I gently declined. If he didn't want things to be *blurry* between us, he shouldn't be paying. I learned he had only budgeted forty-five minutes for me, and I was unimpressed. But as the conversation flowed, I felt myself opening up. It was always so easy with Parker. Nearing the hour mark, he said, "This was far too short," and let me know he'd like to see me again.

I wanted to say no. I couldn't.

We saw each other twice more that week, and I started to feel hopeful. As we spent more and more time together, I began fully lying to myself.

I knew in my heart that if I were "the one," he would have already chosen me. *But what if this time he finally comes around?*

What if he just needed time? I asked myself when I justified another meal together.

All that hope came crashing down when he declined to ask me out on New Year's Eve, even though he ended up at a party just a few blocks from me. I went to bed fuming. I was angry at him, but I was even angrier at myself. *Why am I still wasting my time? What am I waiting for? This is humiliating!*

But then a sweet text message a few days later, and I was back in it. This cycle continued until a revealing conversation in the spring where I learned that Parker and I were not even on the same page about certain relationship fundamentals.* I'd simply assumed we were. I played our interactions back in my head over and over again, realizing we'd never actually had a conversation about this topic. I realized three key ingredients had sustained my imaginationship while costing me invaluable time (not to mention my peace and serenity!): fear, avoidance, and reliance on assumptions.

Once I finally accepted there was no romantic possibility between us (or so I told myself), it felt like Parker was starting to become my best friend. We started working on a couple of creative projects together, each of us marveling at how well we fit in this context. Some days I was thrilled to have such a sweet friend in Los Angeles. Others, I'd lie awake wondering why he couldn't see how great we could be together. I'd wonder, *If we spent enough time together, would our worldviews align?* It was so easy to keep lying to myself. I knew I was on a dangerous path. I just didn't know how to get off it.

---

* For argument's sake, let's say it was around the issue of monogamy vs. polyamory.

Over the summer we reached a sudden breaking point. In the context of a career opportunity, Parker behaved in a way that left me feeling used and discarded. Only then, when things went to the most hopeless place possible between us, did I finally let him go.

It was surprisingly easy to do.

What was harder to reckon with was the fact that I had let another year go by, hoping for Parker to come around. Avoiding conversations about commitment. Swallowing expressions of my deepest hopes and desires.

I vowed to myself that Parker would be my last costar in an unfulfilling imaginationship.

...

It's a Thursday afternoon and I'm on a first date with Reynold, the cute animator I met at a movie premiere. I have no idea, no gut feeling, if he's the one. But he's nice to have lunch with.

"So," he says. "Can I ask you what you're looking for?"

I lean forward, making direct eye contact.

"Something real."

WHERE DID MY FAMILY GO?

SOPHIE

"Quick, inside!" is all I hear before my sister grabs my shoulders and drags me into the closest store.

My brow furrows. "What the hell???"

Siria loosens her grip from my T-shirt and offers an explanation in a hushed tone. "It's Annabel. I didn't think she'd be in the neighborhood."

Okay . . . I'm still confused. "I thought you were cool with Annabel. What happened?"

Siria's eyes are locked on the front window of the shop, scanning for signs of her friend. We're nestled between the toothbrushes and the shampoo. My eyes land on the toothpaste.

When we first moved from Manila to Beijing, I thought that the green leaf on the packaging was mint. Duh, right? My mistake. If you ever see a green leaf on any packaging in Beijing, know that it's green-tea flavored. Never mint. We've been here long enough now that I can read some of the characters on the packaging. I recognize the character for tea 茶 (chá).

Damn, that feels good.

My sister's voice brings me back. "I am cool with Annabel. She invited me to hang out today. I told her I was sick."

"That's *it*?! That's why we're crouching in the aisles like we're fugitives?" I make my way to stand. Siria's done this before—made some bogus excuse for why she can't hang out with a friend because she'd prefer to be with the family. At fourteen I find it bizarre that my seventeen-year-old sister is part of the coolest friend group in school and yet she always wants to hang out with us instead. I had been known to do similar things. But aren't high schoolers supposed to be more mature?

"Something is wrong with you," I say almost under my breath but loud enough for her to hear.

The bells on the door jingle as I push my way back onto the sidewalk.

Siria hid from Annabel like she was doing something illicit. Because in a way she was. How many teens do you know who *hide* from their friends to be with their family?

Granted, we were not your typical family. We moved every two to five years for my dad's work with UNICEF, and China was the latest in a string of countries we had made home. My parents instilled a sense of excitement and adventure into the lifestyle they had chosen, and for the most part it worked. I got used to the rhythm of picking up and moving, and it became addictive. After nearly two years in Albania, when I was around seven or eight, I went to my mother and said, "Okay, where to next?" I became addicted to the novelty of a new place, new people, and a new culture.

Although I had itchy feet, always preparing for the next

adventure, there was also part of me that longed for some stability. I fantasized about living in one place, the same house so we could etch our heights into the doorframe, and I wondered what it would be like to grow up and make lifelong friends. Every time we moved, me and the crop of girls I was leaving behind would swear, "We'll keep in touch! We'll write letters! We'll email!" But even if we started off strong, it always fizzled out once I found a new crew in the place I was settling into.

Penetrating new spaces and cultures over and over again made me adaptable and forced me to develop a knack for finding a connection point with almost anyone you put in front of me. But moving from place to place and continually re-creating networks of support is challenging. When you're uprooted so often, you cling to whatever is constant, and in our case that was our little family unit.

• • •

Over a decade after my sister dragged me into that store, I found myself in the suburbs of Seattle, visiting my husband David's family for the first time after getting married. They live on a quiet cul-de-sac, in a house that I can only describe as quintessentially American—green siding, a big tree in the front yard, and a two-car garage. The only thing missing is a white picket fence. When David was twelve, he moved from the house next door into this one. His elementary school is down the block, his junior high is directly across the street, and when he takes me on an evening walk around the neighborhood, he points out the houses of all his friends, whose families still live there. This is what I had in mind when I pictured the *American dream*.

Halfway through the visit, I sneaked away to chat to my mom

for the third day in a row. I climbed the carpeted steps to David's high school bedroom where we were sleeping, and before I shut the door, I heard my mother-in-law ask my husband, "How do they still have things to talk about?"

My mind goes to the movies I watched growing up. The ones where the protagonist lives in a cul-de-sac with a tree in the front yard and a two-car garage and dreams only of breaking away and making it out of their hometown. I simply can't relate.

I don't have a hometown. My six-year elementary-school experience spans four countries: Israel, Albania, Italy, and the Philippines. My concept of home is placeless; it is anchored entirely in my family.

My mother-in-law's query was not baseless, but we are a digitally connected clan. What we lack in physical proximity, we make up for in FaceTime.

On any given day you can find me on the phone with a family member for the better part of the morning. I call my sister while I do my makeup, make my breakfast, and take breaks between appointments. There have been a number of occasions when I answered her FaceTime from the toilet only to find out she had company! Oops. I've since learned to work my angles so no one can tell where I am. My mom calls while I brew my coffee but bumps me off when a call from my brother intercepts. My brother knows that if he calls her between twelve and two, they'll be chatting one-on-one while he takes his lunch . . . but if his call comes on the weekend, she'll be propped up singing nursery rhymes to distract his daughters while he finishes bits and bobs around the house.

It's not uncommon for me to hang up with my sister only for my mom to ring before I've put down my phone. In fact, my sister called me in the middle of writing this essay. Normally I'd answer, but Nava is sitting across from me, trying to help me get my writing done. Sorry, Siria.

It's not the first time being in touch with my family has gotten in the way of work. Straight out of college I spent three years as a fifth-grade teacher in Brooklyn. My work schedule meant that my family naturally had less access to me, but that didn't stop my mom. She called me while I stood in front of twenty-six fifth graders at the head of the class. Of course, I declined. But when she called right back, I stepped out to answer. *Is everyone okay? Are you hurt? Did someone die?* No, she just wanted to share some of my brother's news with me. This woman had me whispering into the phone in the stairwell outside of my classroom while my students waited for me, just to chitchat.

With plane rides between us, we aren't able to drop by one another's homes, so this is how we manage.

Over time, our closeness worked its way into my sense of self. It was the name tag I'd slap onto my clothes so people knew who I was before I'd even opened my mouth. "Hi, I'm Sophie, and I have a really tight-knit family." But for an identity I had come to hold so dear, it took surprisingly little to shake its foundations.

. . .

It was the storied Mexico trip where I started to realize the shift.

My family is spread clear across the globe. I'm in Los Angeles, where my husband and I are pursuing our artistic dreams under the year-round sun . . . for now. Growing up, I never imagined I would live in the US post-college, and while LA is the promised land for many artists, there is an inevitable end date on our time unless we're prepared to stay in our cozy little rent-controlled apartment until we die.

My sister lives in Scotland, all because of a fateful month at the 2015 Edinburgh Fringe Festival where she met her now husband. When I periodically get on my hands and knees to beg them to move stateside, Ashkan (my brother-in-law) reminds me that his medical training is not so easily transferable and that sun is overrated. "I see Edinburgh in your future," he insists.

My brother, Kalan, the architect and golden child, is in the San Francisco Bay Area. He lives on what we call The Compound with his wife and kids, alongside his brother-in-law's family of four. They share meals and a garden with more fruit trees than you can count. They also pass children from house to house depending on who has a meeting when, which honestly sounds like my child-rearing dreams come true.

After nearly thirty years of moving around, my parents have settled in Italy. They originally moved to Florence for my father's final posting at the UNICEF research center. He has been retired for some years now, so they technically have nothing tying them to Italy except the fact that they decided *la vita* was too *dolce* not to stay.

You can imagine how a spread like the one we have in our family makes seeing one another a little difficult. Add pandemics, pregnancies, and the plans of ten adults into the mix, and getting all of us in one place is a near-impossible task. You don't want to see the tabs our mom has open on her laptop . . . between Expedia, Airbnb, and Google Calendar, it's a miracle her computer is still running. She spends hours each day scrolling through home exchange requests in far-flung places and just as much time trying to convince each family member we *need* to go.

"Dale, Dale . . . wake up. I found great flights to Trinidad."

"Sophie, you won't believe the house I found for us in Paris."

"Siria, what are you doing in November? Sydney is supposed to be nice that time of year. . . ."

"Kalan, we're going to a villa in Morocco, you can either come or not. But that's where we'll be."

She is our maestro; we are her symphony. She tells us where, and we show up. So, thanks to her commitment, we found an open spot in all our calendars post-pandemic, and we took a trip to Mexico together.

I spend most of the year pining for each of my family members, so it was all smiles and giggles from me at the start of our reunion. A regular Rutstein family vacation, except this was the first trip we would take after both my siblings had become parents. David and I had been married for over four years at this point, and despite the many attempts of family and friends to persuade us, we had no solid plans of trying for a baby ourselves (yet). David couldn't make it to this particular family vacation, which made me the only childless person on the trip. Kalan and Milly had their nearly two-year-old in tow, and my sister had her six-month-old.

If there is one place our family thrives, it is in the discovery of a new locale, and Mexico City brought its A game. The women in my family each brought curated lists from our friends who had been to the city before, and we spent a good amount of time huddled over our phones in the crisscrossing streets, cross-referencing lists to find the best spots for coffee, pastries, markets, and beautiful design. We *oohed* and *aahed* at the food, the colors, and the people we met.

We ate churros and guava rolls and marveled at the architecture, our heads craned upward for most of the trip. We took turns pushing strollers through greenways and comforting little ones when the jewel of Mexico City became overwhelming instead of entrancing.

Without me realizing it, we had rolled right into a new stage as a family. I was used to my siblings being my siblings. But like it or not, starting your own family forces you to reprioritize. The dynamic I was accustomed to was changing. Although my sister had been a parent for six months now and my brother for two years, we really hadn't spent any time together in person since then. It became clear on this trip just how much would have to shift to accommodate the new additions to the family.

Late-night chats with my sister after a long day of excursions, I learned, were a thing of the past, especially because my brother-in-law, Ashkan—like David—was unable to make this trip. From sharing a room with Siria as a child to living together in New York, I had grown accustomed to long evenings of whispering and tee-hee-ing with her in the dark. In Mexico her nights were spent rocking and shushing her baby. To her credit, she really tried to re-create what we had had pre-baby. She'd stumble out of the bedroom after getting her daughter down, squinty-eyed with her bun now on the side of her head. She tried to muster up the energy. But we both knew it wasn't quite the same.

"Let's get some rest," I'd suggest. Even though I knew I'd stay up, I had enough heart to put her out of her misery, and to pretend it wasn't just for her sake.

One evening I tried to show my family a movie I had raved about, but my siblings dropped one by one to tend to their babies until it was just me and my mom and dad. My mom had lost interest and started scrolling long before, and at some point between the intro credits and the first turn of the film my dad had nodded off. I felt like the last sibling in a room full of parents.

I was surprised by my melancholy. I was eighteen when we started welcoming new family members into the fold, starting with my sister-in-law, Milly. I remember being moved to tears when Milly and Ashkan married my siblings. At each of their respective weddings I looked out at the siblings and parents of my new in-laws and thought how cool it was that my family suddenly doubled, then tripled. Surely the addition of sweet, chubby children should be even more joyous? I hated that there was even a tinge of sadness associated with the transition that I knew was so meaningful for my siblings.

As this feeling was settling over me, we took a side trip to a remote beach that was a plane ride away from Mexico City. Two nights into our weeklong stay by the beach, a hurricane hit. The villa where we were staying was made up of detached bungalows, many without walls or doors, and with the thunder and lightning the magic of indoor/outdoor beach life was suddenly less magic and more horror. The power was out and the pathways between bungalows flooded.

Milly had gone to bed in her bungalow with my two-year-old niece and the rest of us were stuck in the main hut when the hurricane hit, with no barriers between us and the rain aside from the thatched roof above. There were no walls around the structure, so although we were sheltered from the rain, we could feel the winds and see the downpour in 360 degrees.

And for about an hour, as my sister's six-month-old slept quietly in a safe spot sheltered from the rain, it was the five of us. My brother, my sister, my mom, and my dad. Laughing, screaming, being exactly who we had been my whole childhood.

We used what little battery our phones had left to shine flashlights in the pitch dark. We put a spotlight on Kalan and he brought out his infamous alter ego: Bertha. Bertha was a character he had crafted in his high school drama class, and a performance from her was a rare occurrence in our adulthood. We sat back, giddy. My brother contorted his body to make it look like he had a hunchback and took on the voice of an old, withering lady who referred to herself in the third person.

"Berthaaaaa doesn't like that," he hissed.

Spurred on by the roaring laughter from his captive audience, he gave us just enough to whet our appetites, and no more.

Thunder boomed and lightning cracked. It was clear that the power would not be returning anytime soon, so we staged a democratic vote for who should lead the expedition for supplies. We cackled our way through because, despite the fanfare, we knew all along who would be going. We sent my father off into the darkness to search for batteries.

We joked about how Kalan should buck up and return to his wife and daughter in the next bungalow, but he avoided the treacherous trek through the flooded pathways by assuring us (and himself) that they were safer than he was; he could wait for the rain to subside. But I think he was probably feeling the same way that I was in that moment. Just like an appearance from Bertha, the momentary return to our childhood family unit was rare, and it was worth staying an extra few minutes to draw out as much of the sweetness as we could.

It was bliss. And then it was over. My brother braved the floods and made his way back to his family, back to being husband and father before brother. My sister whisked her baby back down to her quarters after all the commotion, and my parents retreated to their room. We had convened for a moment in our original form, but back to our own bungalows we went.

It hit me then that we had passed a threshold as a family, and now our dynamic would always be shifting. Always in flux from here on out. Our own bungalows calling to us more and more.

I'm not going to lie; I grieved the idea of my family that I had held for so long.

One night I stayed up late, whispering with my parents while my siblings slept with their babies in the rooms next door.

With a lump in my throat and misty eyes, I described my realization to them.

"I feel like we're drifting apart." I tried to keep my voice steady, but there was an undeniable tremble.

My mom commiserated with me. "You're not wrong, honey; there has been a shift. But give it some time; it will settle."

I wasn't quite ready to let go of the family that I had built my sense of self around for so many years. It was like someone snatched something from me and I didn't have time to say goodbye. But there we were, in what felt like a brand-new family.

· · ·

Despite my uncertainty, just like my mom had assured me, my uneasiness did settle—and it settled faster than I expected, during that same Mexico trip. My family rallied all the troops one night and we went out for churros after dinner. My sister and I shared a chocolate dipping sauce. We took turns dunking our churros into the little paper cup while my nieces giggled nearby. The era of nighttime adventures wasn't quite over after all.

With a simple reframe, it's not just that our family dynamic is shifting . . . it's that our family is expanding! And that's incredible.

That's how it's meant to be.

I adore my nieces—I now have four of them. If I were given the opportunity, I would never choose to go back to the family we had before they arrived. I've gotten used to the ever-changing nature of our dynamic. So I was surprised that, when I decided I was ready to start a family of my own and got pregnant, I felt a familiar feeling creeping back in: a looming sense of separation from my nuclear family.

For years before trying for a baby, I daydreamed of how I would break the news to them. When David and I got a positive test, I celebrated the new soul that was growing inside me and immediately started planning how to tell my parents. We lucked out in that they happened to be in California visiting my brother at the time, so what I always assumed would be a FaceTime call would actually happen in person. We made up an excuse to Nava and Penn for why we were suddenly taking a few days off from the podcast (David is our producer and editor), and we made our way up to the Bay.

Over dinner I told my family that I wanted to take a quick clip of them for a video I was making about Ayyám-i-Há.[*]

"Oh, Sophie, no, I'm not camera ready!" my mom protested.

---

[*] The Baháʼí calendar is made up of nineteen months, each with nineteen days, leaving four to five days outside of the calendar called Ayyám-i-Há. Ayyám-i-Há comes right before the nineteen-day fast in March, and it is a time of celebration, joy, acts of service, and generous giving.

My brother chimed in, "Is this going on the internet?"

"It's going to be so quick. No one will even notice it in the compilation!" I assured them.

They finished their final bites while I set up my camera, and I herded them over to the couch. We all piled onto it, spilling over the arms of the sofa and down onto the floor: my parents, Kalan, Milly, my six-month-old niece, David, and myself. My brother's older daughter, Inaya, was asleep in her bed, and my sister across the pond in Edinburgh probably was, too.

I coached the family "Okay! Everyone say, 'Happy Ayyám-i-Há!'"

A scattered "Happy Ayyám-i-Há!" was echoed back to me.

"Okay, let's try one more, say, 'HAPPY AYYÁM-I-HÁ!'"

"Happy Ayyám-i-Há!" they shouted in unison.

"Okay, *one* last one"—I reached for the pregnancy test hidden in my pocket—"say, 'Sophie's pregnant!'" I held it up so they could see.

A cacophony of gasps and screams ensued. My mother let out a shriek that could have cracked a glass. Milly yelled, "WHAT!" and reached over my brother to smack my thigh one, two, three times. My niece burst into tears over the sudden uproar. After calming her, we stood up to hold one another and literally jumped for joy. This would be my parents' fifth grandchild, so despite my excitement, I had worked on not getting my hopes up for how they might respond. Their reaction was better than I ever could have imagined.

Later that night I crawled into bed with David. I wanted to recount the day to savor every minute. We watched the video a dozen times, zooming in on a different family member with each rewatch.

"Look at Kalan's eyes go wide when he realizes what's happening!" I pointed.

"And your dad! His face is priceless," David added.

After a moment of quiet, I noticed the buzz of the evening start to fade. I locked my phone and turned my body to face David in the now-dark bedroom.

Nose to nose I whispered, "That was the last milestone with my family . . . Now that we're creating our own, it feels like I'm losing mine." True, I have been called a drama queen, and maybe I was making more drama out of this realization than was warranted. I couldn't know how I would come to make peace with the evolution that comes with the inevitable rise and decline of generations. I was hopeful about the future and the milestones I would celebrate with my new little unit. But underneath the hope was a sinking feeling that having a child was just the next step in a continual process of growing apart from the family of my childhood, that, in some way, having my own child was a zero-sum transition.

It was indeed a departure. But much like I realized in Mexico, it has also been an expansion.

I understand my siblings so much better now that I have joined them in parenthood, and I am constantly turning to them for advice. I have also found some unexpected connections to my childhood in this new phase of motherhood. As I think about the family I want to create for my daughter, I am often revisiting my own memories of growing up, where I get to spend some time with my siblings in our younger form.

I used to miss out on the present because I was busy looking ahead, but somewhere in the last ten years a switch flipped, and now I have been cursed with a taste for nostalgia. Instead of looking ahead, I'm worried that if I take another step forward, I'll lose what once was. In hindsight, I can see that every stage of life has had its own particular characteristics that are ephemeral. I won't live under the same roof as my siblings again. I won't fall asleep on the couch watching reality TV with my girlfriends again. I won't experience the tingles of dating someone new again. And I won't spontaneously go out to dinner with my husband again (at least for a handful of years). I do find myself missing those periods of my life, but that only means that I've lived a life worth longing for. In fact, I know that I am currently living out a stage of my life that I will add to this list. Soon I will be saying, "I won't rock my baby to sleep again," and I will long for that closeness . . . all the while experiencing something else that I will eventually look back on and miss. Like I said, it really is a curse!

I wonder if the trepidation I feel moving on to new life stages is akin to how some feel about leaving the comfort of their hometown. My mind goes to the Jane Doe living my version of the American dream. She bikes to her neighbor's house to play in the yard before dinner and she walks across the street to her junior high. I look at her life and know that she has it good, but if she dared to leave the picket fence behind for new horizons, chances are she'd find something even better.

Before I could walk or talk I learned the value of leaving your home to embrace new places, new people, and new cultures. The life of a third-culture kid instills a natural flexibility that few "normal" kids will ever know. I can see now that that flexibility is going to allow the closeness of our family unit to continue on in new shapes and sizes. It's time I applied those lessons more broadly.

Loosening my grip on the family structure that once was has

allowed me to grasp new blessings. I am growing to love the new dynamic that my family has adopted, and I am learning that I'm happier when I choose to adapt, to move in harmony with its shifting nature instead of trying to resist it.

But I will also hold space for the sweet family of my childhood. That family of years ago, where we relied on one another, and held on to one another in strange corners of the world, existed for a reason and played an important role in helping us all thrive and grow. With the birth of my own little girl, I now fully realize how inevitable—even natural—the shift has been. But I will also always keep my eyes peeled for the gift of that next thunderstorm that zaps each of us back into our original roles, and I'll relish every moment.

LINEAGE

PENN

I'm not an only child.

I have invoked only child privileges and archetypes throughout the entirety of this book to explain my feelings of isolation growing up, but I do have a half sibling with whom I spent zero years living with. My sister—my father's daughter from his first marriage—was seventeen when I was born, about to go to college, and lived with her mother. She married and had her first child by the time I was seven, making me a child-uncle, which was always a fun little caveat to my only-ness. Our connection as half siblings was our father, and once I was no longer living in the same house as him at twelve years old, my relationship with her would lie totally dormant until I entered my twenties and we reconnected on our own terms (which has been a beautiful and lovely thing).

My father was an only child, and there are almost no other relatives I've known through his side of the family. Three of my four grandparents died by the time I was two, save for my mother's father, an eccentric man whom I knew through stories more than in real life. We traveled to Maryland when he was dying, and his last words to me, as he swam in the liminal spaces of consciousness days from death, were emphatic. He opened his eyes, clenched his hand into a half fist, and said, as though it were the answer to life's most impossible question: "*Do Over.*" He nodded, winked, closed his eyes, and I never saw him awake again. *Do Over* was the name of the short-lived television series I starred in at fifteen (one where I was working twelve hours a day and whose income allowed me to buy copious amounts of weed and an Audi A4 in cash on my sixteenth birthday). He seemed to be saying, "Ya made it, kid." I was a tad embarrassed, as my mother's entire extended family was surrounding us and so many of them knew him much better than I did.

My grandfather served in World War II as a pilot, survived, and then had to live a life afterward like millions upon millions of veterans across the world. Like so many of those millions, substance abuse left a mark on him, his wife, and their kids—my mother and her seven siblings.

The firstborn of the Murphy clan was a pair of twins, Susan and Mary Lou. When the twins were five and my mother was three, Mary Lou drowned. The family arguably never recovered. Dysfunction ruled as their brood grew to half a dozen, and finally the matriarch left the family when my mom was sixteen, without telling anybody. My mother's mother left all her kids. She said that she was going to the movies one night and never came back. After a few days, the children had to alert their father that their mother was probably gone. My mother then had to raise her younger siblings in many ways. I don't know how much any of them knew their mom, who didn't disappear entirely but never reclaimed her status or responsibilities as mother. I certainly never knew her. My maternal grandmother remains to me, and probably to all her children, an enigma. I don't have a clear image of her in my mind; I don't know what she looked like. I met her only as an infant, and soon after, she died on Mother's Day.

Given all this death and estrangement—a family history I neither knew nor understood as a child—I grew up without having much of a place for *family* in my mind. One doesn't know what one doesn't know. In terms of heritage, I had none that I could identify beyond being of Irish and Scottish descent, which didn't mean anything to me because I didn't know anyone from Ireland or Scotland. All I knew of either place were cartoonish tropes, which is all children in America were taught in the nineties. Being Irish, as far as I could tell, had something to do with greenness and Guinness, and being Scottish was much less interesting. No, I was American. That was clear, and yet this, too, meant very little to me. Quite the opposite of American exceptionalism, I felt alien for no single reason I could identify, and I accepted this veiled sense of my place in the world as a standard, just like any child does.

Those early childhood years—my orientation to planet Earth—were in Richmond, Virginia. My parents had met and married in Annapolis, Maryland, before we moved to Virginia when I was two, where they founded a construction company together because it was close to where we lived, and cheap. I remember wandering construction sites as a child. The smell of sawdust and drywall is a deep sense memory that takes me right back to my earliest years, ones I can hardly visualize. There I lived an idyllic suburban life, biking quiet, single-lane streets with the neighborhood boys in a brand-new suburban community that had been carved into the woods only a couple years prior. I had three close friends, two of whom lived less than a minute's walk from my door. There must have been a sense of community there, I suppose, but I can't remember it. It didn't stick.

My final year in Virginia, at seven years old, I switched from a small and unremarkable public school not five minutes from our home to a private school whose commute took me across the James River every day. I carpooled with a boy named Caleb who lived at least twenty minutes away, in what felt like a comparatively rural area. Caleb spoke with a Southern accent as thick and magnetic as Matthew McConaughey's, and like McConaughey (friend of the pod), Caleb relished a good story, many of which he'd tell on the way to school or captivate the class with once we arrived there. He'd laugh and slap his knee with the presence of a man literally ten times his age—one who had been to war, gained and lost lovers, and knew where he came from.

Though I know he wasn't especially tall, in my memory he is huge. He had thick arms, big hands, and the close-cropped hair of a man who had several children and no time. Caleb (a third grader) wouldn't have appeared at all unnatural holding a tumbler of scotch in one hand and a cigar in the other as he hooted and hollered recounting a wild tale about pheasant hunting with his daddy. He had a toothy grin and his round, freckled cheeks framed pale-blue eyes that twinkled with warmth and mischief. He was a good ol' boy before either of us knew what a good ol' boy truly was. I can picture him vividly saying, with a sly wink, "I'm just a good ol' boy." I'm almost certain that isn't a real memory, but I've manufactured it because it works so well.

Caleb and his father participated in Civil War reenactments—all the rage in Virginia at the time—as Confederate soldiers. For them, it was nostalgic, even romantic. Recalling the way these two men [*sic*] spoke about reenacting the American Civil War brings to mind the brilliant Elton John album *Tumbleweed Connection*. Both John and his songwriting partner, Bernie Taupin, have said they regard this album as among their most lyrically and melodically perfect. It's quite a statement, and I actually agree. It's a gorgeous collection of songs, undeniably, and written by two Englishmen who had never set foot in America when they recorded it. It's explicitly not American—it's Americana. It's a fantasy. When I listen to it, I'm transported to a place I would thoroughly love to be, had it ever existed as they're imagining. The songs' protagonists sing about fighting for justice and honor, hitching rides on steamboats, falling in love during wartime, and defending the legacy of their families.

I did not grow up with a sense of family legacy, nor a sense of where I came from. Where *did* I come from? What *is* a legacy? The remoteness of my family history—my genealogical vacuum—has always induced me to feeling somewhat foreign no matter where I am and intensified my feelings of only-ness as a child despite being a brother, an uncle, and a son. The irony of success in my field as an actor is that, for all the literal fanfare it brings, it creates its own sort of vacuum. Despite being known in some manner by millions, my experience of solitude was only magnified as I matured through my twenties under the specter of celebrity. Have you not heard? Being famous can be so *unpleasant*!

Having written one-third of this book (and willing to take all the credit), it strikes me that my life experience has been one of spending time between extreme environmental opposites—solitude and celebrity—which have the same internal condition. Quite simply, the feeling of being alone. Imagine, if you will, for a moment: a man nearing forty years old, with a smattering of gray in his beard and upon his temple, with a wife and two children, and who, after nearly twenty years in the spotlight, is attempting to describe (at book length) his experience of isolation growing up without using the word "lonely." Why would he do that? What could warrant such mental gymnastics? Why would he, even for a moment, second-guess himself in the use of such a universally employed word to describe a universal experience? What could possibly exert such a malevolent force upon his psyche that he would, in his loneliness, be barred from even naming it?

Yes, I was a lonely boy. As a man, this sensation deepened. I hadn't created my own loneliness as a child, but it had become my responsibility to acknowledge, understand, and break the cycle as an adult. I'm still learning how to do this. What I offer now—after having dragged you through the mud with me—is the light at the end of the tunnel, one that I couldn't have imagined while I was growing up.

There are two lights, actually. One is standing right in front of me. My wife and I have a four-year-old son, whose bed I am writing from because every other room in our four-bedroom Brooklyn apartment is occupied. On this bright and frozen Sunday afternoon in February, I couldn't be alone if I tried. My sixteen-year-old stepson—the other of the two lights—is in his room next door, where I can only assume he is bathing in the designer cologne he has recently purchased for himself. (If you're wondering, yes, providing guidance and watching him traverse his own adolescence over the last few years—the exact same years I've been cohosting *Podcrushed*—has been poignant, serendipitous, and a tad psychedelic.) Across the hall, my wife is answering emails, like any professional on a Sunday, as she sits in our bed. And my mother is in the office that acts as our guest room, where she has been reading *Winnie-the-Pooh* to the four-year-old who has now come to find me. He is standing at his dresser in a plain T-shirt and dark sweatpants with a white drawstring that he wisely refers to as "teenager pants" because he sees his beloved big brother wear pants like these almost every day (with slip-on sandals, no matter the weather). His little back is turned to me as he opens every drawer. Deciding he hasn't found what he needs, he closes every drawer, and every time he shuts one, he mutters, "Shoot."

This is the point of the exercise. He's not really looking for anything. He wants to perform for himself (and me) the act of being a little bit frustrated and being able to express it. When he does this, he says it exactly as my mother does. It's an uncanny resemblance. No one else in our family says "shoot." What's more, he doesn't do this through the mysterious, generational osmosis that can happen within a family, where a child exhibits behaviors of a parent or grandparent or uncle or aunt without knowing it, or possibly without ever having witnessed it. What my son is doing is intentional. He is consciously repeating what he sees my mother do all the time, because he sees her *all the time*.

I have endured long periods of estrangement from both of my parents, just as they did theirs, and for reasons that might be superficially various but which are ultimately the same. We've not known love well: how to use it or what it is for. We've not known that it is a verb, or how to use it as a tool. Until I entered my thirties—my thirties!—I didn't know that it required attentive cultivation. Now that my four-year-old son has taken his pants off and his tiny bare bum is squarely facing me (still wearing his shirt), I can smile and appreciate that the family I belong to is finally learning something about love and how to make it work. I'm learning how to break the cycle.

When my wife was pregnant with our first child, we lost it very early on. We tried and got pregnant again. We made it a bit further, but the first time I was ever in an obstetrics office for a sonogram to see my child in utero, there was no heartbeat. This was our second loss together, a time when it did not feel as though the cycle would break. My wife and I neared separation, as many do after losses like that, largely because we felt so isolated in a culture that doesn't talk much about these things or know how to support those going through it. Seeing our still baby in that tripped-out black-and-white sono-imagery is a dreadful memory I can't shake every time we go for a sonogram now. As of this writing, my wife is pregnant, and we have identical twins on the way.

They will make it four lights, soon. Today marks the conclusion of the first trimester. This is when, in America, it is finally advisable to tell people about a pregnancy because the first trimester is reportedly where the most miscarriages happen. Elsewhere, like in Puerto Rico, where Nava grew up, people tell everyone as soon as they can, so friends and family can pray for the little ones on their way—to encourage them. Nava told me this weeks ago when I shared our news with some hesitation. She also reminded me of something Dr. Laurie Santos (actual happiness expert) said on *Podcrushed* when we were interviewing her: in any kind of loss, your grief is never abated, prevented, or reduced by not allowing yourself joy and excitement while you actually have the thing. So enjoy it.

Speaking of things, my son has left the room and returned triumphantly, now wearing brightly colored Hot Wheels underwear patterned with neon-red race cars and a long-sleeve Nike jersey that says in large and patronizing block letters: "WATCH AND LEARN." My wife would never purchase clothing so full of microfiber plastics. I know this is my mom's doing—a gift from Gaga. My son pats the crotch of his underwear and says with wonder, "I found where to put my penis."

I'm glad it's easy now. That journey will only become more difficult, son.

Before I can say anything, he bounds out of the room and down the hall where I can hear my mother shuffling to meet him. She's currently losing her little sister, my aunt, to dementia—a slow and painful loss by degrees. My mother has been the oldest of her generation for several years now. It admittedly doesn't take much to bring her to tears these days, but when she first saw pictures of our twins in utero, she wept and noted poignantly, "My life started with twins, and it's going to end with twins."

Not all cycles need to be broken.

AFTER THE WORLD STOPPED SPINNING

NAVA

We often think of coming of age as something limited to our adolescence. But if coming of age represents a maturation of a kind, certain seminal experiences can usher in our coming of age well into our adulthood. There is no greater coming of age in my own life than the one brought about by the sudden, unexpected passing of my mother.

. . .

When I was a child, I would sometimes ask my mom about my grandmother, Sabiheh, who died before I was born. Sabiheh was very sick when my mom, Farahnaz, was born, and for the first few years of her life, another woman helped raise my mom. When my mom turned fifteen, Sabiheh was diagnosed with breast cancer, and the doctor said she would likely die within the year.

"When I heard the news I prayed and begged Baha'u'llah not to let my mother die before I married. I couldn't stand the idea of being without her, totally on my own. I begged Him to let me keep her until I could start my own family," my mother would say.

My mom married when she was twenty-nine years old. Sabiheh died the following week, in my mother's arms. She lived for fourteen years with aggressive breast cancer, defying all the odds. The doctors had no medical explanation for it.

"Are you afraid of death?" I asked Mom after she told me this story the first time, when I was ten years old.

"Not at all. I'm very excited to die, actually. I can't bear the thought of losing your father, so I'm very hopeful that I will die first. And I miss my mother so terribly. I really want to see her again. I'm very curious about the next world, too, and what it will be like. But of course I will miss you and Zhena so much. You will have to try very hard not to be sad when I die. It will affect me too much if you're sad, I think. You must try to be happy for me and the new adventure I'll be on."

"Okay," I said. "I'll try very hard not to be sad."

I had no idea what I was talking about.

. . .

On July 30, 2014, I had a dream that my mom and I were together. She slipped into bed and patted the spot next to her. "Nava *joon*, *bia*,"* she said in sweet Persian tones as she motioned me over. I slipped into bed next to her, and she caressed my arms and hugged me and told me she loved me so much. I dreamed of us in her bed together the whole night. When I woke, I thought about how sweet and unusual this dream was.

---

* *Joon* means "dear," and *bia* means "come" in Farsi.

My first thought was, *Tell Mama; she'll be so moved!* But I had to be at work at 6:40 a.m. and told myself I'd call her over a lunch break. Two weeks earlier, I had moved to Tempe, Arizona, to start a new job as middle school director at one of the most successful charter schools in the country (unlike teachers, school administrators don't get summer break). Even without the time off, though, I couldn't get over how amazing my life was and how things were turning out more beautifully than I could have ever imagined. I couldn't wait to tell my parents how incredible everything was.

At around ten a.m., after I'd done the morning rounds, I was suddenly seized with a spontaneous, unexplained panic. *Something is going to happen to Mommy.* I walked out of my office and into the parking lot, walking to the back of the building hoping to avoid any students. I slid down a wall and started weeping.

"Baha'u'llah, if You're taking my mom away from me, You need to prepare me, because I'm not ready." After a few deep breaths, I tried to brush my fear away. *You're being ridiculous. There's nothing wrong with your mom.* I picked myself back up and went about my day. I had a meeting after work that night, so I decided I'd call home the next day and tell my mom about the dream then.

The following day was really busy at work, and I didn't get a chance to call. I went to the mall after work to pick up some new running shoes[*] and decided I would call my parents after a community gathering I was attending that night. I went to the Tempe Bahá'í Center and thought about how lucky I was to be part of such an amazing group. I noticed a missed call from my dad and decided to call him once I got home, because I hated being on my

---

[*] To this day, it kills me that I went shopping instead of calling home. Kills me.

phone and driving. While I was driving home, my sister called, too. I let it go to voicemail.

I walked into my new studio apartment, spacious and beautiful, humming to myself and wondering what finishing touches remained. Maybe a potted plant.

I hit my voicemail and listened to my sister's message. "Nava, you need to call Daddy right now. It's really important." She sounded serious and worried. I wondered what was wrong.

I called him right away. "Hi, Daddy!" I said cheerfully when he answered.

"Nava, your mom died," he responded.

No "Hello," no "Sit down, I need to tell you something . . ." Just the blade to my chest, sharp and swift. My dad had just watched the woman he loved die suddenly, unexpectedly, in his arms. He was not equipped to deliver the news with Novocain.

I screamed. Like a movie cliche. "You're lying! YOU'RE LYING!"

"Nava, sweetie, I'm so sorry. I'm not lying." His voice cracked and he started crying. "I don't know how else to tell you. She died thirty minutes ago."

My mother had asphyxiated. She either died of a pulmonary embolism or a major heart attack, but either way, she couldn't breathe over the course of twenty agonizing minutes. (My father has tried to share the details with me several times but I simply cannot bear to hear them, so I'm still not entirely sure what happened, why the ambulance took so long, and what my poor father endured in those final, brutal moments of her life where she did, indeed, suffer.)

The moments after the call are kind of a blur. I called my sister next and we sobbed together. Both in shock. Both unsure what was next. My sister, so strong, agreed to be the one to call our relatives and let them know. After those calls, some of our family members started calling me to offer condolences, and the tears would start again. After about an hour of this, I switched into pragmatic gear. I called my boss and left her a message letting her know I would be flying home for my mother's funeral. I texted my friend Natasha and told her I would be missing an important gathering that weekend because my mother died. (I offered no further details.) I booked a ticket home for the next morning.

Natasha called me right away and asked me if she'd read my text correctly. Then she asked if she could come pick me up so that I could spend the night at her house. She didn't think I should be alone. Her husband, Drew, and cousin Ashkon didn't think I should be alone, either. They both sent their love, unsure what else to say in the moment.

I told her it was okay. My flight was early and I needed to pack. But she asked if she could come over and pray with me. "Okay," I said. Thirty minutes later, at midnight, Natasha, seven months pregnant with twins, was at my door with our other friends Soheila and Chandra in tow.

They all hugged me.

We all cried.

Chandra informed me she was spending the night. "Okay," I whispered again. "Thank you."

We said prayers for Farahnaz, my mom. (*Was she still my mom?*) Chandra sang. Natasha and Soheila squeezed my hands. I smiled, my cheeks dry. I told my friends I was happy for my mom. Her soul must be rejoicing to be reunited with her parents, her brothers who'd both died the summer before. "I'm happy for her," I repeated. I meant it.

Soheila and Natasha eventually left. Chandra helped me pack, and then we crawled into bed. An hour later an intense wave of grief hit me. I climbed out of bed and walked into my closet, closing the door behind me. I sobbed until I finally fell asleep in there, curled up into a tightly wound ball, until Chandra woke me up two hours later to drive me to the airport. I made it through security, and when I reached the gate for my flight, I found a seat in the corner and let myself go.

I wept and wept until my head throbbed from dehydration, and still I wept some more. An older gentleman had been watching me closely in the waiting area and finally approached. He sat down next to me and tapped my shoulder gently. "Excuse me, miss, I hope you don't mind this intrusion, but you look like you're in a lot of pain. Is there anything I can do to help you?"

I glanced up at him, gathered my strength, and whispered, "I just found out my mom died."

"Oh, sweetie, I'm so sorry." He motioned for his wife, who had also been watching me carefully, to come over. She sat on the other side of me.

"Her mom died," he told her gently.

"Oh dear," she replied, her voice full of sorrow. "Can we pray with you?" she asked.

"Yes, please." I barely opened my eyes.

They held my hands and bowed their heads and we all prayed silently together.

I have never forgotten that couple or their kindness. It was one of the diamonds that shone in the darkness during that terrible time.

Once I got home, I woke up feeling like I'd been hit by a truck every single day. My body ached and I had no energy. I was in real physical pain, and every morning it would take me a few minutes to remember what had happened and why I felt like this. Every time I remembered, it was a fresh heartbreak. I truly had no idea human beings could feel so much pain. I felt betrayed by life—*how could we be built to feel so much?* It was unfathomably cruel.

And the hardest part of that week was yet to come.

As part of the Bahá'í rites associated with death, one washes the body of the deceased and wraps it in a white shroud. The deceased also wears a ring that says "I came forth from God, and return unto Him, detached from all save Him, holding fast to His Name, the Merciful, the Compassionate."

When my mom was twenty-nine—just a year younger than I was—her mom died. She used to recount how meaningful the act of washing her mother's body was to her. I knew that I would wash my mother's body, too.

My dad, sister, and I drove over to the morgue in relative silence, late at night. I stared at the trees whizzing by and the stars shining down, wondering what vistas my mom might be seeing from wherever she was. We arrived at the morgue and were told what to expect. We were handed gloves and pointed in the direction of where her body was being kept. I froze in place. My dad and sister walked ahead of me, but I couldn't move. Suddenly, I was crashing down on the floor, gasping for air, my heart beating incredibly fast. I was having a panic attack.

"Nava?" My sister had come back, noticing I hadn't followed behind. Then she spotted me on the floor, in the middle of the lobby.

"Nava!" She rushed over to me.

"I can't do it, Zhena," I cried. "I can't, Zhena, I can't. I don't want to see her like that. I don't want to." My sister hugged me and brushed my hair and told me it would be okay and we were going in there together. I breathed in and out and finally stood up. "Okay, I'm ready." We walked in together.

It was very hard to see her body on the table. Her eyes were open but she was gone. My mom was so spirited, her eyes always sparkling with innocent mischief. Her playfulness was often on display, boundless love shooting out of those tender brown eyes. In that moment, if I ever had any doubt, I became sure of the fact that human beings have souls, and it is our souls that give us life. This was my mom's body, but this was not my mom's essence.

Farahnaz was a spiritual being and this was her sacred temple. We washed it as such. I'm very thankful that my sister helped me overcome my panic attack because washing my mom's body was an incredibly sacred experience for me. I felt so fully the truth of those words on her ring. God had given her to us, and now we were giving her back to Him. We washed her body with rose water, and I shampooed and conditioned her hair, grateful that it was the one thing about her that was the same in death as it was in life.

I kissed her head, her cheeks. I kissed her goodbye and thanked God for letting her be my mother.

· · ·

It's been ten years since my mom died. Sometimes I don't know how I survived the bottomless pit of grief. The first year after Mama's death, I woke up about once a week screaming, remembering she was gone. About once a month I woke up crying, imagining my father dying, too.

Not a single day has passed since her death that I have not prayed and asked God to give my father an exceedingly long life. I pray that when it's his time, I'll be ready (and then I always whisper, *I'm not ready! Please don't take him!*) and that I'll have the chance to say goodbye. Sometimes I'll stare at him and my eyes will fill with tears. He usually pretends not to notice, but once in a while he'll squeeze my hand and his eyes will tear up, too.

I suppose a gift of my mother's death is that I don't take my dad for granted. I prioritize time with him over most other things, and I let him know multiple times a week how much I adore him, what a wonderful father he is, and how grateful I am to be his child.

But loving someone that intensely is also terrifying. I am fearful of the day he's gone. I simply can't imagine going through that kind of pain again. My father is my tether. What happens when I lose the greatest source of unconditional love in my human life? My dad is in his eighties, and when he dies (hopefully at one hundred) no one will think of his death as tragic. But it will be a tragedy to me.

I think the extreme loneliness and isolation of the modern age can make death a particularly brutal phenomenon. Some pain is too heavy for one person to shoulder by themselves; we *need* others to carry it with us—to surround us, shower us with love, food, care, questions, attention.

My impulse after my mom died was to be alone. Two weeks after she passed, hardly anyone was reaching out to check on me, anyway. It felt like, *your two weeks are up, you've had your tears, keep it moving.* I perceived that both my professional community and my religious one—where I actively volunteered on a number of rigorous development projects—felt that my grief was a distraction they didn't have time for. That feeling only increased my despair.

A few months after my mom died, my boss at my charter school actually told me that the fact that my mom had died during the first week of school was "an unfortunate setback" that had cost me important bonding time with new students. I suppose if she had died the first week of September, it would have been more *fortunate*.

A co-committee member on a service team I was part of once followed me out of a room when I'd excused myself to go outside so I could collect myself in private. This was one month after my mom died. She asked me what was wrong, and I replied that I missed my mom so much. She asked, "How can we reframe this so that it's a joyful thing?" *Why does it have to be a joyful thing? I wondered.**

I think what I needed most the months after my mom's death was friendship, but I also needed friends who weren't trying to rush me out of my grief. One well-meaning friend frequently reminded me that men liked "happy women," and I should try to present "more cheerfully." I needed friends who would give me space to cry. Who would ask me to share my favorite stories about my mom. I don't recall being offered that space, so I'd like to claim it now. Here is one of my favorite memories of Farahnaz.

· · ·

One day, when I was in ninth grade and Zhena was a senior, my mom came home shaking.

"Mommy, what's wrong?" Zhena asked her.

"A man tried to assault me at Glidden." Glidden was a paint store.

---

* "Wondered" is too soft. Fumed, raged, seethed . . .

"WHAT?!" We both shrieked. "What do you mean, 'tried'?" Zhena added.

"I was walking back to the car with my wallet tucked in between my arm and armpit, and I was carrying a can of paint in each hand. This man came up very close behind me and grabbed me to detain me. Then he reached for my wallet."

"Wait, did he have a knife?" I asked.

"Or a gun?" Zhena shrieked.

"I don't know," my mom continued. "I didn't see anything. But I slowly put the paint cans down, turned around, and grabbed him. I dug my fingernails into his arms, looked him in the eyes, and said, 'No!'"

Zhena and I exchanged glances.

"She gave him the evil eye," Zhena proclaimed.

I knew exactly what she meant. When Mom was angry or thought you were in the wrong, she had this stare that put the fear of God into you.

My mom continued. "I guess I was digging really hard into his skin because he started bleeding, and he actually begged me to let go of him. *'Por favor! Por favor!'* When I let go of him, he ran away from me."

"Mommy, are you crazy?" I cried out. I was angry at her for endangering herself. But also impressed.

"Mommy! Your wallet is not worth it!" Zhena scolded her.

"That's not the point. This man wanted to take advantage of me, and I was not going to let that happen."

Mom proceeded to put her wallet down on the counter. Of course she'd managed to hold on to it. She asked us to help her with the paint cans.

"You know, when Mommy started this story, I didn't think I'd feel bad for the mugger," I said.

"He had no idea who he was messing with," Zhena added.

My mom pretended not to hear, but a little chuckle escaped her lips, and her eyes twinkled while she opened one of the paint cans to begin swatching samples.

That was Farahnaz.

The most fearless woman I've ever known.

• • •

As I come to end of my essays, it's hard to know how to bring things to a close. I wanted to end on this note of death, but my editor insisted that would be a bummer for readers. I countered that anyone who listens to *Podcrushed* already expects me to be a bit of a bummer, but in the end, my editor won. (Hi, Molly!)

Likewise, as I was putting the finishing touches on this particular essay, the Palisades, Eaton, and countless other fires broke out in Los Angeles, and I evacuated to San Diego in search of healthier air. On the drive down I wept. During the full two-and-a-half-hour drive, I felt like I was in a true state of mourning. Mourning for our planet. Mourning for the coast. Mourning for a vision of my life at forty that has very much not come true.

When I got to San Diego, I began working on my revisions, and I had to decide which of the many stories of my mother to include as the closing one for this collection. I chose the one about the guy who tried to mug her. *Why that one?* It was honestly the first one that came to mind. When I called my sister to run it by her and make sure we remembered it the same way, we both laughed as we relived that day. We marveled at our fearless mother.

I think that's why I chose it. I think that's why I wanted to end my collection here.

We're living in frightening times.

I, at least, am frightened. I think the current moment, the current order, calls for a lot of courage. A lot of strength. I believe that each and every one of us will need to level up. We'll all be called on to display a certain level of fearlessness in our lives as we fight for the ones we love, and for the strangers we've never met. As we fight to maintain our values, and as we fight to cultivate integrity in a system that often rewards corruption.

These are scary and dangerous times, but they are also days of portent and potential. We have the opportunity and the responsibility to cultivate new relationships: with our inner selves, with our neighbors, with our very own resources. We need to write a new social script. We know that every choice we make leaves a trace. That our actions are impactful. That being guided by fear or by courage will make the difference in whether our lives are driven by reaction or by intention. The choice is ours: to retreat into fear or to step boldly into a future shaped by hope, connection, and shared purpose.

I'm so grateful to my father, Tommy, to my mother, Farahnaz, and to my sister, Zhena—for instilling me with these values and for making my past so joyful, my present so stable, and my future so hopeful. I love you three the most. Whatever the world has in store for me, I am already eternally grateful to be a part of your tribe.

DECISION DAY

SOPHIE

When I was twenty-seven, I came across a video that illustrated the rate at which female fertility declines over time. Bummer, I know. When I found the video, I knew I wasn't ready for kids yet, and even though I was firm in that decision, it left me feeling anxious. I got the sense that I was nearing the end of my "prime," and that if I wanted kids, I had to pull the trigger. Fast.

From the earliest age, I was sure I wanted to be a mom. At two I carted baby dolls around the house in a mini stroller. At six I called four-year-olds "cute," like I was their auntie. I have always wanted to have babies, but the desire to mother crystalized in high school.

At sixteen, I started regularly babysitting a six-year-old girl named Frederika. She had bright blond hair and an adorable Dutch accent. Weeks before I began looking after Frederika, her mom had passed away very suddenly, leaving the whole family (her brother, father, and herself) in a dazed state. Because I was the first female figure to step into a caring role after such a devastating loss, Frederika immediately became attached to me. She had a constant need for physical touch; if we were coloring at the table, she would scoot her chair close enough to mine so that she could rest her hand on my forearm. If we were watching a movie, she was nuzzled into me. If we were on the playground, she would choose a game that required us to hold hands. I welcomed the physical closeness; I soaked up Frederika's love and I poured my own into her. Being a surrogate mother for her in the wake of her own mother's passing remains one of the most fulfilling roles I have ever taken on, and it confirmed my need to nurture and to hold.

The year that I took care of Frederika, my friend Emily asked where I saw myself at twenty-five and we exchanged our visions. Sitting behind the Domino's Pizza across the street from school, between bites of garlic knots and cheesy bread, I told her I saw myself married with three kids.

And yet, at twenty-seven I was baby-less, watching a video on the decline of fertility.

David and I had gotten married four years before, and any time I was asked when we would try for kids (because, try as they might, people cannot prevent themselves from asking), I always said, "We'll have kids in two years."

It doesn't take much math to realize that we were essentially lying to everyone, including ourselves.

At sixteen it was so easy to say with such conviction that I wanted to be a "young mom," whatever that means. But as the goalpost approached, I continually pushed it back.

I thought that seeing my older siblings have kids would encourage me. Like, surely, I would be so obsessed with my nieces that I wouldn't be able to *not* have kids. And even though I *was* fully obsessed with my nieces, if anything, it made me want to wait longer. Being an auntie is one of the greatest roles you can inhabit in this life, and it satiated me. Also, frankly, it gave me an inside look into how hard parenting is. The decision consumed me. Part of me wished that I would find out one month that I'd gotten pregnant by accident. That way the choice would be out of my hands, and if I ended up regretting it, at least I couldn't blame myself for making the wrong choice.

I felt like I'd been shrunk down to the size of an ant, sitting on the ball of a pendulum, swinging from side to side. One minute I'd be cooing to David about how I wanted a small, cuddly human in my arms STAT. And the next minute, I was wondering if I would ever want to have a child at all.

I simply liked my life too much. I think if I had had kids early, I wouldn't have known what I was missing, but I had gotten to a point where I was attached to my life. I was attached to my time. Uninterrupted time to create, slow and intimate mornings with David, the flexibility to spend hours becoming friends with my neighbors. I knew I had it good.

I wondered if I would ever get to a point of feeling ready. Whenever I asked the question, the response was always "No, you'll never be ready. You just have to go for it." How could that be the common consensus? The idea of jumping headfirst into a lifelong commitment without feeling ready seemed too risky to me.

I wondered if maybe there was a secret group of parents who really hated the decision they had made but couldn't admit it. I've since come to find out that there is, in fact, a subset of parents who do regret their decision to have children. There is a whole side of Reddit for regretful parents to exchange thoughts and experiences: r/RegretfulParents. Enter at your own risk.

Desperate to know more, I called my sister to ask for her perspective.

Siria, I know you are obsessed with your daughter. But I need to know . . . do you ever wish you started later?
Absolutely not, she said.

How did you know it was the right time?
I always felt drawn to babies. I loved children.

But there was a particular shift after being married for a few years. Even just seeing babies, on social media or in real life, I was overwhelmed with this feeling of desire and longing. To hold a little being in my arms and to have that little being be something that my husband and I shared together. And that feeling just got stronger and stronger.

I have that feeling, too . . . but I have that feeling, and then I don't have that feeling.
Yeah, but that's the same with so many things that are scary in life. You'll have the feeling and then you'll get scared, and you'll think about all the things you love about your life currently—

So . . . I interrupted her, **that's just how it's gonna be?**
She chuckled. It is, kind of. I think to a certain extent it is always going to feel that way. You will be entering a new phase of your life. Your life will change. But one of the beautiful things about life, and about the capacity of human beings, is that we can constantly grow. Becoming a parent

is one of the surest signs of that. You become capable of so much more than you could've ever imagined, and you do it because it has to be done. Your capacity expands because it just has to. I think that's one of the bounties of having children. You, yourself, go through a process of transformation. And that's, at the end of the day, what life is all about. It's about constantly transforming, becoming better. Children really do that for you.

Her words were comforting, but still, it took me nearly two years after that phone call to make up my mind.

Whenever I thought about the conflict of having children, I saw myself perched on a fence, trying to decide where to land, while the fence grew, and grew, and grew, separating me further from my target. Despite my sister's calm encouragement, over the two years I descended into less and less certainty.

Though I do remember one pivotal moment of clarity. It came, believe it or not, after watching the penultimate episode of *This Is Us*. Rebecca, the matriarch of the Pearson family, is on her deathbed, and she's looking back on her life with memories flooding in of all her children and her children's children.

It dawned on me that the memories I would be looking back on, on my deathbed, hadn't happened yet.

The bond that I shared with Frederika all those years ago suddenly kept bobbing in and out of my head. I didn't want to delay the future anymore. I wanted to start living in the memories that I knew I'd be cherishing at the end of my life.

Of course, children are not part of everyone's life path. It goes without saying that you can have an exceptionally full and rich life without children. I know that firsthand, because I was living a life that was filled to the brim with joy and meaning before I had my daughter.

Now that I've chosen which side of the fence to jump to, and I've landed on my feet, I can say that I don't have regrets. That's not to say becoming a parent is not life altering. Before I gave birth, I had fantasies of my baby simply fitting into my life. There is some value in that way of thinking, but now I laugh at the naivete. Parents make countless sacrifices and shifts to meet the needs of their babies hundreds of times a day.

Do I miss the piles and piles of time that I had before having a child? Of course.

Do I fantasize about afternoons with nothing to do? Sometimes.

Do I daydream about twenty-four hours at a hotel just to draw the curtains and rot in bed? Absolutely.

But what is that worth in the scheme of things? I decided, at least for myself, that it wasn't worth enough. I don't think we're meant to stay in one phase forever, even if we could somehow do that. Of course, you will have moments of longing for other stages of your life than the one you're in, but that is true after any transition.

I miss being reckless with my friends in high school, exploring abandoned buildings around Beijing. I miss living in New York City in my early twenties, hopping on the subway without a reason to rush home. I miss the dating stage with David, the mystery, the intrigue.

But you have to move forward in life and trust that you are going to keep living the phases that you will one day look back on.

Anaïs is going to teach me hundreds of things I don't yet know. For now, she is constantly pulling me back to the present moment.

I spent the first twenty-odd years of my life always looking forward, moving on, rushing. And I've spent the last few years perpetually looking back, missing what was, and wishing I had cherished it while I had it. My sweet baby hasn't even formed a sentence, but she has achieved the impossible: keeping me tethered to now.

I am settling into my life, trying to allow it to play at 1x speed. Not too fast, not too slow. But I do still catch myself imagining the future sometimes, wondering how many siblings we'll give to Anaïs, hoping we'll one day afford to buy a home, dreading the thought of losing my parents, among other musings. And I hope that in several decades, looking back on my life, I'll be able to say I cherished what I had, while I had it.

On a follow-up call with my sister, I asked her to try to sum up the experience of parenthood, and she gave an answer that I think is worth some thought.

Follow-up call with Siria:
When I think about parenthood, I think about life in full saturation. Everything is more intense. It's like a montage in an Oscar-nominated film. You never forget that scene, that montage of the fullness of life, with all of the characters experiencing the highs, the lows, the tests, the beauty, the joy, the pain.

Not everyone's montage will have children included, and many will prefer it that way. But I think it's a worthwhile thought exercise, no matter what vision you have for your life. What do you want your montage to include? When your memories are played back, flickering past, what do you hope to see?

THIS IS WHERE WE SAY GOODBYE

We fondly refer to the listeners of our podcast as *crushies*. It's so tempting to come up with a nickname for the readers who stuck around, but is that too familiar?

Check yes ☐ or no ☐.

In lieu of a nickname—and we can't say "Dear Reader" (thanks, Taylor)—we'll jump straight to: THANK YOU.

Thank you for being our therapists as we unpacked all that childhood trauma. Please contact our editor, Molly, to provide a billing address.

Thank you for bearing witness to our lives. Together we explored first loves, first heartbreaks, earth-shattering losses, the allure of fame, finding ourselves in faith, and longing for transcendence. We questioned the labels and traits that at times anchored so much of our self-worth: from seemingly superficial attributes like weight to seismic ones like race. We reminisced about the friendships that defined us and recoiled remembering the relationships that wounded us. We parsed through family relationships and the ways they shaped us—how they lifted us up, let us down, and sometimes left us searching for closure.

We subtitled this book a collection of essays on love, loss, and coming-of-age, but some of us have not yet had a great love, others have not experienced enormous loss, and none of us would claim to have fully "come of age."

As we write this, we are in the thick of it all—still caught between who we were and who we are becoming. We are unfinished, in process, and still learning how to navigate the complexities of our lives. A couple of us are raising new humans (how can babies raise babies, we keep wondering!), stepping into roles that demand more than we thought possible. Others are standing on the precipice, uncertain of what's next, but hopeful that in the waiting, we, too, will bloom.

In the end, this collection is a snapshot of a journey that isn't complete—our stories still unfolding, our lives being written.

We hope that bearing witness to the times we fell flat, turned left when we should have gone right, broke our own hearts, and somehow kept making the same mistakes again and again helps you feel a little more grace toward every version of yourself—the young kid who was figuring it out and the adult who might still be operating from an outdated script.

We also hope we made you chuckle at least a few times. If not, blame Molly. Please send her an invoice asking for your money back.

Actually, blame Penn. We couldn't have written this book without him, but we could barely write it with him. Trust us when we tell you that you'll never meet a man more adept at making a hard deadline soft.

Penn is protesting that his cut is not big enough for us to use this sign-off but . . . it's just . . . right . . . there . . .

XOXO,
Nava, Sophie & Penn

ACKNOWLEDGMENTS

When we set out to write *Crushmore*, little did we know that, more than writing a book, we were holding up a mirror. At times, our younger selves peeked back at us with tenderness. In other moments, we were forced to face reflections we might have preferred to leave in the past. The process opened unexpected doors: to our twelve-year-old selves and our childhood friends; to the cities that made us and the forces that shaped us; to old wounds that hadn't quite scarred over.

Of course, the memories of childhood and youth sometimes have little to bear on what actually happened. Nonetheless, they constitute much of how one feels about themself, and so, memories matter. Drawing on ours throughout this book (corroborating as much as we could whenever possible), it was impossible not to collapse the people who appear in each story into supporting characters who are unable to defend themselves from biased representation. While this is true of all stories, nowhere does the risk of subjectivity loom larger than in one's personal narrative.

For this reason, at least, we changed almost all of the names that appear in the book. And to the real people behind those names (most of whom know who they are), we thank you for helping us understand ourselves. We can only hope that we've played a similar role in your personal story.

To our editor, Molly Gregory, who has more patience than anyone we have thus far met, thank you for pushing (and sometimes dragging) us to the finish line; we are indebted to you. To Matt Attanasio, your grace in the face of unanswered emails gives us faith in the future of humanity. And to the rest of the team at Gallery Books and Simon & Schuster, we appreciate all the work you put into bringing *Crushmore* to life.

To Abby Walters, Josh Lindgren, Andrea Weintraub, and the rest of our team at CAA, as well as Doug Wald, thank you for your critical moments of assistance.

ACKNOWLEDGMENTS

PENN

A majority of my writing work had to be completed during my wife's first trimester when she was pregnant with our twins, and it was a special cosmic challenge that these two periods coincided. No one had to deal with more difficulties in writing this book than she did, and no one needed more support than her while it was happening. Domino, I love you, and I thank you infinitely for the unconditional love you give to my inner child. To my stepson, Cassius, who was navigating his own sixteen-year-old experiences across the hall from my office as I wrote and whose adolescence unfolding in real time has been a surreal inspiration throughout *Podcrushed*—I love you, and enjoy the man you're becoming more every day. To Boone, my four-year-old who won't be able to read these pages for about a decade, you single-handedly made completing this book the most arduous task of 2025 and I wouldn't have it any other way. I hope you never stop interrupting my work. To my mother, whom I badgered with a series of fact-checking calls way too late in the process and who is the only person on the planet who could be responsible for any belief I have in myself—there is no way to thank you. I love you. Finally, to Nava and Sophie, whose partnership I have valued so much these last five years—thank you for creating a space where I could learn to be lighter. You both carry gravity with grace, and I'm happy to be telling our stories together.

SOPHIE

To my husband, David, thank you for your steady support through the long days and longer nights of writing. While I clicked and clacked at my keyboard, you carried what I couldn't in every other area of life. None of this would exist without you!

To my father, thank you for reading every page I placed in your hands, without hesitation or complaint. Your willingness to lend your eyes and ears gave each story a place to land before it made its way into the world.

To my mother, your honest opinion has always been my north star. Thank you for helping me mine the past with clarity and care.

To Penn and Nava, thank you for being the kind of collaborators who challenge, and inspire. You didn't let me quit, even when I was convinced I had nothing meaningful (or coherent) to say. Whether or not the readers thank you for that remains to be seen.

And finally, to my baby, Anaïs, googoo gaga, I love you!

ACKNOWLEDGMENTS

NAVA

To my friends at the Episcopal Cathedral School—it was more dramatic to tell the stories of things that went wrong. But you were the best classmates, friends, and humans I could have ever hoped to experience my formative years with, and I love you all so much.

Josh, thank you for being the first set of eyes on any of these pieces. Your feedback helped propel me forward when I needed momentum.

To my dad, Tommy—you are barely in these pages, which makes no sense, because you are one of the great loves of my life. That's what you get for not traumatizing me as a kid.

To my sister, Zhena—thank you for being my friend through it all. You are the first person I go to with my heartbreaks, my triumphs, and my life. I adore you.

To my maman joon, Farahnaz—you know my heart. I love you eternally. Thank you for giving so much of yourself to bring me into being and mold me.

Penn, Sophie—thank you for the last five years. I've had the time of life with you. You weren't part of my past, but I can't imagine my present and future without your friendship and influence.

ABOUT THE AUTHORS

PENN BADGLEY is an actor, director, producer, writer, and podcaster best known for his starring roles in the CW's *Gossip Girl* and Netflix's *You*. He lives in New Paltz, New York, with his wife, two children, and two dogs.

SOPHIE ANSARI is an illustrator, video creator, and podcast host. She moonlights as a community organizer, tallying many hours each week volunteering with children on her block and bothering her neighbors until they offer to feed her. Sophie lives in Los Angeles with her husband, David, and their baby.

NAVA KAVELIN is a writer and producer based in Los Angeles. She and Penn Badgley cofounded a production company, Ninth Mode, together in 2020, and Nava is CEO. Prior to her work on *Podcrushed*, Nava taught at Tsinghua University in Beijing, and was a researcher and writer at the United Nations.